WE OWN THIS GAME

WE OWN THIS GAME

A Season in the Adult World of Youth Football

Robert Andrew Powell

Atlantic Monthly Press
New York

Published simultaneously in Canada
Printed in the United States of America

Portions of this book originally appeared in Miami *New Times*.

FIRST EDITION

Library of Congress Cataloging-in-Publication Data

Powell, Robert Andrew.
We own this game : a season in the adult world of youth football /
Robert Andrew Powell.
p. cm.
ISBN 0-87113-905-7
1. Youth league football—Florida—Miami.   I. Title.
GV959.53.M53P69 2003
796.332'62—dc21   2003044327

Atlantic Monthly Press
841 Broadway
New York, NY 10003

03 04 05 06 07   10 9 8 7 6 5 4 3 2 1

To my parents

Contents

Contents

Pop Warner strives to make the game "fun" for all boys and girls. Coaches must constantly keep in mind the ages of the participants. The program stresses learning lessons of value far beyond the playing days of the boys and girls involved, such as: self-discipline, teamwork, concentration, friendship, leadership, and good sportsmanship.

With such goals in mind, and by providing an opportunity to participate in an organized, supervised environment with emphasis on maximum safety and participation, Pop Warner Football offers young men and women a unique experience.

—Pop Warner Rule Book

Preface

I moved to Miami ten years ago with the typical take on the city: transient, poor, Spanish-speaking, dangerous, hot as hell in the summer, still a bit too hot in the winter. Compared with the Chicago suburbs of my youth, Miami might as well be Manila. Concrete houses painted pink line streets littered with old refrigerators and broken bottles. Chickens roam free. Rusty freighters overflowing with stolen bicycles chug down the Miami River en route to the Dominican Republic, often returning with bricks of cocaine hidden in their bowels. Even the lawns look different, with hearty blades of grass sharp enough to cut skin. Angry fire ants thrive in that grass, waiting to bite the legs of anyone naive enough to picnic.

There are people older than Miami. As a young city, Miami maintains a frontier spirit, welcoming anyone motivated to stake a claim. The city's emergence as more than a boom-and-bust tourist backwater didn't begin until the widespread installation of air-conditioning, just fifty years ago. A massive influx of Cuban refugees, peaking in the early eighties, transformed a redneck outpost into the capital of Latin America. While Cuban exiles and their offspring now constitute the largest segment of the city's population, countless other nationalities pepper the stew: Haitians, Brazilians, Nicaraguans, even Russians and Italians, along with more than a few transplants from such exotic ports as New York and Pittsburgh.

Like most people, I came to Miami to make a buck, in my case as a journalist. The newspaper where I worked asked me to cover city politics. For several years I monitored a Miami government less interested in crime and trash removal than it was committed to toppling communism in Cuba. While public pools sat dry and homeless entrepreneurs stripped the aluminum bleachers from stadiums the city neglected, Miami's leaders funneled tax dollars to exile aid groups and to no-show jobs for Bay of Pigs veterans.

"None of us actually thought we'd stay here for the rest of our lives," Cuban-American City Commissioner Willy Gort told me, "so we didn't pay much attention to improving the neighborhoods." Bribery scandals, quasi-comic fiscal mismanagement, and a mayoral election in which at least one dead man voted forced Florida's governor to commandeer the city. Prior to the takeover, Miami's lone black commissioner was caught on tape wiring a $25,000 kickback to an offshore bank, crowing into a hidden microphone perhaps the greatest last line ever: "Let them trace that, huh?"

Even before his arrest I'd viewed Commissioner Miller Dawkins as a buffoon. He'd held office for years and, as far as I could tell, hadn't done much of anything for his constituents. Race riots in the eighties left the black community starving for investment, yet Dawkins used his office to steer housing contracts to his unqualified friends. Those houses never appeared, but few people noticed. With the political focus trained on Fidel Castro, the needs of Miami's black community were easy to overlook.

I overlooked black Miami myself. In my preconceived notions of Miami, I—an "Anglo" transplanted from the Midwest—hadn't factored in the black experience. Most of what I knew came from television: Crime-obsessed local stations broadcast the aftermath of drug-related shootings, with bombed-out storefronts providing the backdrop. The reputation of the black Liberty City neighborhood wasn't helped by the murders of several German tourists unlucky enough to have taken the wrong exit off Interstate 95.

Then I saw a football game, and my perception changed. It was a high school game, the state semifinals. Two Miami teams played in a communal stadium located on a campus of the junior college. Florida is known as a breeding ground for speedy wide receivers and ferociously fast linebackers. And in Florida, no one plays the game better than the high school teams from Miami. Local teams have won six of the past nine big-school state championships. Many of the athletes from those schools stay in-state to play college ball for Florida, Florida State, and the University of Miami, national champions all, three of the most successful college programs in the country.

The game that night more closely resembled major college football than the high school stuff I'd seen growing up. Yet what impressed me more than the play on the field was the action in the stands. There were 18,000 people crammed into the stadium, and several thousand disappointed fans milling about the parking lot, unable to buy tickets. The bands at halftime danced and shook with infectious energy. And—this was hard for an outsider like me not to notice—everyone in the stadium was black. Everyone. It was my first real immersion in black Miami, and it made an impression on me. Hopelessness was not the dominant vibe. That football game was a celebration.

And it wasn't uncommon, I learned when I began attending other games. Carol City versus Central. Southridge versus Homestead. All the top teams are black. Even Miami Senior High, located two blocks from Elián Gonzalez's temporary home in Little Havana, fields a roster of primarily black players. The level of support showered on these teams is astounding. The regular-season meeting between two top schools, Northwestern and Jackson, took place in the Orange Bowl stadium before more than 46,000 fans. *Forty-six thousand.* For a game with nothing more than pride at stake.

Such mind-boggling attendance figures are not new in Miami. Even more people attended a game played forty years ago between then-powers Miami High and Coral Gables. Football at that time, in what was then the segregated Deep South, was an all-white sport. Blacks played too, but off the radar. An annual Thanksgiving Day game called the Turkey Bowl received light coverage, primarily from the black press. Yet today blacks dominate football in Miami. Something has shifted. Something significant.

A few months after I'd started attending the occasional high school game I ran across a blurb in a newspaper's sports section. The

Pop Warner football championships had been played the previous Saturday. Pop Warner is the Little League of football, played by kids between the ages of six and fifteen. A team from Liberty City had won a championship in one division. A team from Goulds, located among the farmland in the southern half of the county, had won another. I noted the attendance figures. More than 6,500 people had turned out for the championships. To watch kids as Lilliputian as 65 pounds play football. How deep did this passion for football reach? I wondered.

I decided to find out. On assignment for my newspaper, I spent the following autumn with a team of eight-year-old football players from Gwen Cherry Park, in Liberty City. Gwen Cherry is surrounded on all sides by public housing projects, yet every game that season was a festival featuring not only football but barbecues and music and neighborhood girls dressed in their flashiest outfits. Most of the fans who attended Gwen Cherry games, I discovered, were born in Miami and had lived there longer than anyone I knew, including most of the politicians I covered. While even Miami's mayor was wondering when he'd flee Miami for his native Cuba, these people considered themselves Miamians to the bone, and considered football their greatest pride.

"Somebody a long time ago came to the idea that this—football—was the very best way to show that we could make it out, that we could rise above the slave mentality, segregation, and really be what we want to be," the uncle of a Gwen Cherry player told me. "With the generations that have passed since then, over time, things have gotten stronger and stronger. It's not a *part* of the culture now. It *is* the culture."

At Gwen Cherry Park I saw much to admire. The team's coaches sacrificed three hours of their day, five days a week, to help single mothers raise young boys into men. I saw a depressed community proud that its boys could do something better than anyone else. I saw aimless kids find direction in the discipline of the game.

Yet I also witnessed the corruption of sport at its infancy. I saw the team's best wide receiver—an eight-year-old—recruited to play after starring the previous season at a different park. I saw a culture of winning so pervasive that fans assaulted the coaches after the team's only loss. I saw parents living through their kids, dreaming of NFL paydays while their sons were flunking out of school. I saw big money gambled on the games. I saw kids learn that stellar play can earn them cash rewards from drug-dealing boosters.

Although I spent a full season with that team from Gwen Cherry, I was never able to immerse myself as deeply in the subject as I wanted to. My newspaper always needed more stories, and I had to contribute my share. I wrote about mob-connected con artists, shady car dealers, and, of course, the young Cuban rafter who dominated the news in Miami for more than a year. But even as I worked on other assignments, I yearned to revisit the world of youth football. Why is the sport virtually all black? Why is it taken so seriously, so young? What does passion for football say about Miami? What does the passion for youth sports say about America?

In a world where high school athletes have started bypassing college to jump directly to the pros, the attention paid to youth sports grows ever more astonishing. The Little League World Series is televised live on ABC; Vegas takes bets on the game. The Pop Warner Super Bowl—the national championship held every year in Orlando—is broadcast on ESPN. The trickling-down of professionalism from college to high school and now onto the sandlot has fostered ugly consequences. A Little League pitcher in the Bronx employs a fake birth certificate to lead his team to a title. A hockey father in Massachusetts kills a rival father in a fistfight.

When one Miami Pop Warner coach, suspended by the league for running up the score in the national championship game, filed suit to get back his volunteer job, I saw an opening I couldn't resist following.

In the spring of 2001 I quit my job at the newspaper and committed myself to covering a full season of the Greater Miami Pop Warner football league. I followed one team of past national champions, the 95-pound Liberty City Warriors, from the first day of registration to the last day of their season. I attended every practice, often sitting on a lawn chair with the parents and eating a dinner of fresh conch sold from the back of an ice cream truck. I attended every team meeting and game. Off the field I visited kids, parents, and coaches at their homes and schools and work.

I didn't limit myself to covering just the Warriors. At a park hidden in the suburbs an hour south of Liberty City I found Raul Campos, the Darth Vader of Pop Warner coaches, a title he brandishes with delight. Campos, who is white, has won two straight national championships with a team comprised entirely of black players recruited for their speed and other athletic gifts. I also regularly attended practices of his team of thirteen- and fourteen-year-old players. On more than one Saturday night I sat with Campos in his living room watching boxing matches on his big screen, drinking beer with his assistant coaches, and exercising my painfully bad Spanish on his parents, both Cuban exiles.

I talked to people on the periphery of the game, including politicians, boosters, cheerleading coaches, and rap musicians. I studied the historical reasons why the black community is so isolated in Miami, then I watched a mayoral election showcase the isolation perfectly. At the end of the season I drove five hours up the Florida Turnpike to Orlando, to Disney World and the Pop Warner Super Bowl.

When I started the project I'd planned to spend most of the season getting to know the kids who play the game. Why do they play? What pressures are on them, if any? Yet, after I returned from Orlando and began thumbing through my notes, I realized that in talking to the people most invested in Pop Warner football, I'd spent most of my time talking to adults.

The Pop Warner Super Bowl was played on a field of scrupulously maintained grass, as might be expected at Disney World. The hash marks and end lines lay as straight as the squares on a checkerboard. The Tifway 419 Bermuda turf sat level and smooth and glowed a green so inviting it practically shined. It was a perfect lawn, a perfect playing field. But it was also located in Florida. As anyone from the Sunshine State knows, there are fire ants in that grass. And they bite.

Prologue

The sign appeared in late April. A sandwich board painted crayon yellow and stenciled in black spray gloss, the lettering different heights and fonts. "Football" printed as tall as a toaster, "Registration" in letters smaller than house keys. "Liberty City, Optimist Club," a phone number. Grains of plywood peek through paint eroded by a tropical sun. For three months a year, every year for the past eleven years, the sign has stood on a patch of grass along Northwest 50th Street across from Hadley Park. However crude its construction, the sign conveys a message easily understood: Football season is upon us again. As if everyone doesn't already know. As if everyone isn't already waiting.

🏈 🏈 🏈

In the bedroom of his house in Liberty City, Brian Johnson's two computers whir and hum. All afternoon he's bounced from one machine to the other, scouring the Internet for a novel new play or a nugget of coaching wisdom his competitors may not have come across. Ink-jet perfume rises from a printer. Out rolls yet another page of the incredible new, full-color playbook Brian and his assistants have spent the off-season assembling. Sha-nise, Brian's eleven-year-old daughter, knocks on the door playfully, knowing her father will ignore her. His wife of thirteen years seeks permission to change the channel on the living room TV from ESPN Classic, which is replaying a college football game the Miami Hurricanes won a decade ago.

"Un-uh, baby," Brian calls back. "I'm watching that, too."

Brian stands five-feet-eight inches tall, 225 pounds, with skin the color of strong tea. Once a week he shaves the receding hair from his head, leaving him with a round globe roughly the same shape as his torso. He's soft, not fat, and he dresses for comfort in the uniform of Liberty City: a Nike T-shirt cut extra large, baggy shorts hanging down to mid-shin, a pair of shiny black sneakers—Nike, of course, the only brand his teenage son will let him wear.

Brian started coaching the Liberty City Warriors eight years ago, when his son joined the 65-pounders—Pop Warner football teams aren't divided by age but by weight, which ranges from 65 to 145 pounds. Brian volunteered to run his son's team, but coaching the 65s, even as an assistant, was deemed too important a position for a rookie. Instead he was allowed to assist the coaching of the six-year-olds, a job he held for three years.

"At that level you teach them how to put on their helmet, basically," he recalls. "There isn't a lot they can do." In time, long after his son moved up in weight, Brian joined the coaching staff of the 95-pounders, working first as an assistant, then as the offensive coordinator of a team that won a national championship in 1998. This will be his first year as a head coach.

"I got to try this," Brian says. "I went to clinics, I did scouting. I went on the Internet looking up plays. I collected any info I could find on anything. I want to do it the right way, my way. Maybe I suck, but I got to try. I wouldn't be a man if I didn't aspire to be head coach, to run my own team."

In the bedroom with Brian are his new offensive and defensive coordinators. Coach Pete will run the defense. He's a small man with a wispy goatee, braids in his hair, and a low and booming voice left over from his days in the Army. Pete was an assistant with Brian when the 95-pound Warriors marched all the way to Orlando and Disney World and a national championship.

Anthony Beasley, Brian's best friend, will run the offense now that Brian's ascended to the top job. Like Pete, Beasley served a tour in the Army, as a policeman. He works as a debt collector, calling people on the phone to recover money owed to the Ford Motor Company. Even when he talks about football he maintains the rapid-fire patter of a salesman, albeit a humorless salesman of extraordinary intensity. "He believes what he believes no matter what other people say, and that's why I like him," says Brian. Whenever a colorful page of Xs and Os rolls off the printer, Beasley tucks it into a clear plastic protector, then files the page in the master playbook. As the three-ring binder begins to bulge, Beasley can barely contain himself.

"No one has ever seen anything like this before," he says. "No one."

Beasley is a lifelong fan of the Georgia Southern Eagles, a powerhouse college program that runs one of the most complicated offenses in football history. Ever since he learned he'd be in charge of Liberty City's offense this season, Beasley has planned to teach the Georgia Southern system to his Warriors, who range in age from eight to eleven.

"No one at this level has ever tried this before," Beasley says, serious as a mortician. "I don't see any reason why we can't win it all this year. Our motto is 'If You Believe It You Can Achieve It.' And I honestly believe we are going to win the national championship."

Images of Disney World pop into Brian's head. Epcot Center and the Magic Kingdom. A spongy green gridiron. An unlucky team from Connecticut or somewhere unprepared for the superior football played in Miami. Another national championship.

Brian is thirty-five years old. His two kids are smart and polite and progressing nicely through school. His wife, a nurse at Jackson Hospital, is the love of his life. His day job driving a delivery van is stable and relatively high-paying. And now, finally, after years of biding his time as an assistant, he's the head coach of his own Pop Warner football team.

"Orlando," he says, letting the name hang out there for a few seconds as if it and not Miami were the Magic City. "Man, there's nothing like it."

● ● ●

Twenty-five miles southwest of Liberty City, in a subdivision of waterfront homes divided by white ranch fences, Raul Campos documents his legacy. He's sitting in one of his spare bedrooms, which he has converted into a video production studio. Outside a sliding glass door, a geyser sprays water ten feet above an artificial lake stocked with bass. Inside, on a monitor in front of Campos, images of the rural black neighborhood of West Perrine tumble past: men huddled on a corner; blown-out trailer homes on lots strewn with trash. Some of the houses, to Campos's disappointment, feature lawn ornaments, pruned shrubbery, and minivans parked in the carport.

Campos waves his hand and his assistant coach, Santaris Lee, hits the play button on a classic rock hit by the Animals. A steady bass groove vibrates from a set of stereo speakers flanking the eighteen-inch monitor.

> "*In this dirty old part of the city, where the sun refuse to shine, people tell me there ain't no use in trying.*"

Campos leans back in his leather chair and allows himself a satisfied smile.

"We're showing where the kids live, you know?" he says. A cluster of public-assistance town houses streams by, each painted a vibrant mango. Candy-colored playground equipment occupies a wide swath of mowed grass. "And this song's appropriate, 'Ain't no use in trying' and all that. The neighborhood looks clean because they keep it painted and stuff but, boy, that's a rough place to live. We wanted to really get into it and film some dope deals and stuff, but decided against it. If you go there at night you find it everywhere."

Campos is finishing a promotional video of the Raiders' past two championship seasons. With the sound track set, Lee rewinds the master tape to the beginning. On Campos's signal, Lee hits the play button. A black screen. The words "Field of Dreams" fade in, in white lettering. The shrill beginning to the theme from the TV show *Mission: Impossible* shatters the silence. Crashing horns, a pulsating bass. "Dum dum da dum . . ." A legend unspools, white letters on black, bottom to top in *Star Wars* style:

During the 1999 and 2000
football seasons Coach Raul
Campos and Santaris Lee
coaching at Palmetto
Optimist Club put together a
football team that won every
championship there was to
be won . . .

Dum dum da dum . . .

including back-to-back
national championships at
Disney World Sport Center.
They used an offense
designed by Coach Campos
which they named
"The Whip" offense. . .

Dum dum da dum . . .

and simply dominated the
entire youth football world,

not only in Miami, but in the
entire nation.
They amassed a 30–0–1
record in just two seasons.
As a team they accomplished
more than any other team

Dum dum da dum . . .

ever had. And in their quest
made Palmetto Optimist
nationally famous by
showing everyone in the
world where the best youth
football ever played came
from. They left a legacy which
will live long after they are

gone.
So that every future Raider
player who plays in the
"Field of Dreams" can have
not only something to be
proud of, but also something
they can set their goals by.
For History cannot
Be changed!

Cue the first visual: a shot of mostly empty Palmetto Field. The
screen fills with blurry images of yellow grass, a lonely pair of bleachers, and a South Florida sky so blue it could be computer-generated.
A crashing guitar chord from the Animals' downbeat ballad "When
I Was Young" sets the mood. Campos leans in to record the voice-
over, the whiskers of his beard nearly scraping the thin microphone
wand.

Prologue

"This is the nationally famous Palmetto Optimist football field," he says in his best Voice of God. "Not much, is it? Just a few old bleachers, an old clubhouse, a scoreboard, and a field. But don't let the looks of that field fool you. This field is sacred. That is because it is a Field of Dreams. Yes, that's right: dreams. This is where it all starts for hundreds of young boys. Right here. Young boys with nothing but raw talent and dreams. Dreams of running, catching, tackling, or perhaps even throwing that last-second touchdown pass to win the Super Bowl of Super Bowls."

Campos pauses as the camera pans away from the empty bleachers to reveal a pair of concrete posts for the lights, a few parked cars, and a grassy berm in the distance. On the field, five white boys from the upper-middle-class neighborhood that surrounds the park play catch. This is unfortunate, for their presence undermines Campos's attempt to make the field look sufficiently ghetto.

"Yes, dreams," Campos continues. "It's sad but so. Sometimes those dreams are the only thing they have to get them through the hardships of everyday life.

"Hello. My name is Coach Campos. The film you are about to see is real. No fiction here. No drama. And no comedy. Just the hard facts of life. A film about a bunch of young kids who grew up just around the corner, a place called West Perrine. Who set out to prove they were winners. Kids who refused to lose. And on the way I've—er, they've—already accomplished more than any other team ever has. That is to win back-to-back national championships. Along their quest they made Palmetto Optimist Field nationally famous by proving to all the other teams in their region where the best youth football ever played comes from. It wasn't easy. As a matter of fact it was hard. Very hard. And this is how they did it."

The camera sweeps 360 degrees, to the bleachers, to the berm, to the kids playing catch, to the scoreboard, to the bleachers and round again, over and over until a crashing cymbal finally ends the song. Segue to the tour of West Perrine.

Campos and Lee have worked on this tape for a month so far, picking the music, splicing the shots, writing the narrative. After the trip to the neighborhood from which Campos recruits the blazing speed that makes his teams so exceptional, the tape proceeds to thirty-five minutes of highlights from nearly every Raiders game played over the past two years. Despite Campos's narrated insistence that winning back-to-back titles was "hard, very hard," the endless string of victories don't look particularly difficult. A Palmetto running back peels off an 80-yard scoring run. A safety returns an interception untouched for a touchdown. A wide receiver drags a would-be tackler ten yards for yet another score. Scoreboard shots show playoff wins of 24–0 and 34–0.

Campos's Raiders haven't lost a game in two years. Each season he keeps the same players from the year before and moves up with them a weight division. Two years ago Campos won the national championship at the 110-pound division, one level heavier than Brian Johnson's Liberty City Warriors. Last year Campos won with the older and heavier-still 125-pounders. This year he plans on winning at the 145-pound division, the midgets, the oldest players and the toughest competition in Pop Warner.

Because he stays with one group of boys as they age, and because the roster of this year's team is largely set, Campos has time to work on his memoirs. In addition to the video he's also completed a draft of his autobiography, which he has entitled "Winning It All." He hopes that, with one more championship under his belt, he'll be able to find a publisher for the book. The goal is to cement his reputation, as he's said more than once, as the greatest youth football coach of all time.

The tape culminates with footage from Campos's most recent national championship win. In Orlando, at the Disney Wide World of Sports Complex, on the same perfect green field where Brian Johnson's Warriors won their title in 1998. Palmetto Raiders throw and catch touchdowns in a 32-point shutout of an overmatched team from Connecticut. As Queen lead singer Freddie Mercury celebrates another one biting the dust, Campos pulls out his script and hits the record button one more time.

Prologue

"When we get through this year we will be the best youth football team to have ever played," he tells the microphone. "And I mean *ever*. Our legacy will live long after we're gone. Coaches, it's up to you. It's up to you to get our players ready to rumble. Pride and glory don't come easy. Together we will repeat. Long live Palmetto Raiders Field. Long live the Field of Dreams. By all of us pulling together we will win."

🏈 🏈 🏈

Nine-year-old Diamond Pless is a billboard of name brands: a Polo T-shirt, red. Saucony running shoes. Hilfiger socks. Even so, his most distinctive feature is natural: narrow eyes that give him a slightly reptilian look. This afternoon, as the heat rises off the parking lot of the public housing complex where he lives, he fans his face with his tiny hand. When his younger sister laughs at his pantomime he throws her a quizzical look. He's not trying to be funny. He's just hot.

Diamond's uncle, Durell, is leading Diamond through a preseason football practice. "Let's go out there and do what we do every day," Durell says, rolling out into the sun in his wheelchair and holding a beat-up plastic football in his left hand. He has to shout to be heard over the roar of cars speeding downtown on Interstate 95. Durell points the ball to the north and Diamond runs to the north. He points the ball south and Diamond runs south. He points at his chest and Diamond sprints toward him. When he points the nose of the ball at the ground, Diamond backpedals as fast as he can, his sneakers skidding on the pebbly blacktop when he tries to stop.

"Okay, six seconds. Good," imparts Durell, looking down at a cell phone he uses as a stopwatch. "Do it again now, faster."

When Diamond runs, his pink tongue tickles his chin. His face is passive, unsmiling. The exercises, which would drain a grown man in minutes, come effortlessly to him. He is a good athlete, but he has been a disappointment to his coaches on the Liberty City Warriors, primarily for his lack of concentration. One coach, familiar with Diamond's performance in previous years, already seems to have written him off. "Diamond, he be like a girl," the coach scoffs days before the start of the 2001 season. "He be more into clothes and stuff than he be into anything else."

Diamond gets some of his fashion sense from his uncle. Durell sports a Technicolor tropical shirt, baggy blue jeans, and sky blue Nike running shoes, which perch on the footrests of the wheelchair he's been confined to for seven years, ever since he was shot during a feud with a rival drug dealer. Gold gleams on his wrist. A sizable pendant shaped like a padlock dangles from his neck. His hair is a braided crop of neat rows weaved into zigzagging right angles. Dark black tattoos stain the brown skin on both forearms. When a good play by Diamond prompts Durell to flash a wide smile, he reveals four gold teeth studded with glinting, clear stones arranged like playing card suits. He is the father figure in Diamond's life.

"Every day before practice we'll be out here an hour or two," Durell explains when he lets Diamond take a breather. "We don't do nothin' that gets him real tired. We work on the basics, the fundamentals. A lot of what's wrong with Diamond is he's athletic—he has all the athletic capabilities—but he isn't focused. And I want him to play. I don't want him to rot on the bench. I don't want him kicked off the team.

"This is serious," Durell continues, referring to football in general. "It wasn't like this with our parents back when we were growing up. Back then you maybe see parents at a game but not out at practice like I am every day. Now parents see a guy staying right here in this building, [wide receiver] Marvin Minnis from Florida State University, he made it out of here. You see people from your community actually make the NFL it gives you hope. You push 'em a little more."

Durell looks at Diamond, who cools in the shade of a nylon canopy hung over a bank of mailboxes. Diamond will play this season for the 95-pound Warriors under coach Brian Johnson. This will be his fourth year of Pop Warner football.

"I really feel like he's living out my dream," Durell admits. "A lot of people probably feel the same way about their sons. Just look at the little kids at the park. How many kids at four and five years old really want to play football? It's parents. It's pressure."

●　●　●

Even now, on the last day of registration, Mark Peterson feels the heat. Some of it is weather-related, for late July is an especially cruel time to live in South Florida. What outdoor activity there is usually takes place at night. Fashionable diners on Lincoln Road in Miami Beach won't sit down for sushi before 9 P.M. Out in the suburbs, recreational softball players field grounders under the cooler illumination of halogen lights. It's the time of year when a stick of chewing gum left in a parked car needs only a minute of midday sun to wind its way down a dashboard in a river of liquid sugar.

It's not even noon and already the sun chars the brown grass of Tamiami Field, a broad public park carved from the suburban sprawl west of Miami. Little League baseball players, regretting their choice of sport, fan themselves with oversized leather mitts. A pitcher wipes his brow with his forearm. One of the more pragmatic team mothers sits in her car with the air-conditioning cranked. Peterson rolls his black Ford F-150 pickup into an empty spot next to her. He shifts into park and cuts the engine. With one hand he twists shut a plastic bottle of Diet Coke resting between his knees. With his other hand he grabs a soft leather briefcase. He opens the door and hops down onto the pavement. Just like that the season changes. Enough baseball. Who's ready for some football?

Peterson is the commissioner of the Greater Miami Pop Warner football league, arguably the most successful local Pop Warner program in the country. In the last three years teams from Miami have won seven national championships. In 2000 alone, teams from two different Miami parks achieved undefeated seasons, each for the second season in a row. One of those teams was the Palmetto Raiders, coached by Raul Campos. The other team, from Suniland Park in suburban Pinecrest, won its national championship in a game televised nationally on ESPN.

Prologue

That Suniland victory gnaws on Peterson as he walks across the parking lot. The Sundevils pasted a previously undefeated team from Washington, D.C., by a score of 56–6. So lopsided was the victory that the Pop Warner national office, asserting the Suniland coach had deliberately piled it on, suspended him for a season. The coach has sued to get his job back. Newspapers and national magazines mocked the lawsuit. Peterson realized he can no longer sidestep the direction his league is heading.

Suniland is one of several Miami parks that have begun fielding successful teams built around the talents of boys—almost exclusively black boys—bused or driven to practice each day from as far as an hour away. Some are recruited by the coaching staff. Some recruit themselves, knowing that if they play for certain teams they'll maximize their chances of winning a trip to Disney World: a week's vacation and all the food they can eat and a game played on national television.

In the off-season, Peterson attempted to address recruiting, which he feels is at the root of the Suniland problem. He drafted a bylaw stating that, without a specific waiver from the league, kids now have to play their football in the park closest to their home. If a ten-year-old boy lives near Silver Blue Lake Park, he must play for the Northwest Falcons. If his mother picks green beans in the open fields southwest of Homestead, her son must wear the baby blue jersey of the Florida City Razorbacks. The aim is to prevent boys from being exploited.

"Everyone likes to win," Peterson says. "Hell, I like to win. It's just that football at this level shouldn't be so much about winning. I think they're forgetting that this is supposed to be a recreational sort of thing."

Stepping inside the concrete-block Tamiami community center, Peterson blinks repeatedly while adjusting to a cool darkness. Bulletin boards display hand-painted warnings about the dangers of drug use. Off the main hallway, a meeting room teems with activity. Parents float among folding tables in search of the right place to deliver registration forms. Aspiring defensive ends dart from one end of the room to the other, squeaking sneakers on the linoleum floor, shouting in high voices that have not yet changed.

"What position you playing?"

"Really? I want to be a linebacker."

"My mom thinks I should be a running back but I want to throw the ball."

"What's your weight?"

Peterson is wearing denim shorts, a weathered Polo shirt, and a floppy baseball hat embroidered with the logo of last year's Pop Warner national championships. Under the hat flows a mullet of graying hair. At a table pockmarked with strips of masking tape he pulls out a thin stack of paper and a fistful of ballpoint pens, laying them down next to his soda and his cell phone. He looks up to find a mother waiting for his attention.

When the boundary matter came up for a vote, fifteen of sixteen parks favored precincts. Only one park voted against: Suniland. After losing the vote, Suniland officials promptly complained to the county government, arguing that everyone has a right to play sports at any public park they want. The county agreed and struck down the boundary rule. Suniland—and other parks like it—were given the green light to recruit as they please.

Which makes Peterson's presence here kind of meaningless. Since he can no longer deny access to a park, Peterson decided that everyone who plays outside their natural neighborhood must sign a waiver. It's nothing more than a tracking mechanism, or maybe just a statement of good intentions.

"Is this where I sign to transfer my son to another park?" the mother asks, cradling a baby in her left hand and reaching for a pen with her right. She says she wants her son to play for Palmetto, even though she lives in the northwest corner of the county, a rush-hour commute of up to two hours each way.

"And why do you want your son to play all the way down there?" Peterson asks.

Prologue

"Because I want him to," she replies. Peterson looks at her for two or three seconds. He lets out an overtly theatrical sigh, flips the form around, and asks her to sign on the dotted line.

"Fine with me," he says, looking past her to a lengthening line of mothers waiting to sign the same form.

🏈 🏈 🏈

Located on the southern fringe of Liberty City, which is the heart of Miami's black community, Hadley Park features two illuminated baseball diamonds, tennis courts, basketball courts, and an Olympic swimming pool named after former city commissioner Miller Dawkins, recently released from federal prison. A sweeping grass field dominates. Less conspicuous are the remnants of a way-out-of-fashion concrete roller-skating rink. In the center of the park, under the canopy of a banyan tree, stands a jungle gym large enough to give a toddler an anxiety attack. A new community center rises on the north border, along 50th Street. When it is finished a year from now it will house an auditorium, rooms for after-school study, and the offices of the Liberty City Optimist Club, parent organization of the Liberty City Warriors football team.

Late into the last day of registration, two barbecues the size of oil drums puff smoke into the leaves of a ficus tree. Atop a picnic table sits a bag of paper napkins, paper plates sealed in plastic wrap, squeeze bottles of barbecue sauce, and a cooler overloaded with sodas in strawberry and fruit punch flavors. Ketchup, mustard, and relish are in the mix, as is a bonfire-sized pile of chicken wings and drumsticks. Still more chicken—and hamburgers and hot dogs and even a few slabs of ribs—roast on the twin grills, their fat dripping onto coals with an audible sizzle.

"This is what we should have been doing every year," says Sam Johnson, biting into an ear of corn so watery he sprays a ten-year-old reaching for a soda. Sam (no relation to coach Brian Johnson) founded the Warriors eleven years ago. He continues to oversee the day-to-day operation of all eleven Warriors football teams, plus cheerleading and, in the off-season, basketball and baseball programs. "We should have picnics so that everyone in the neighborhood can get involved, kind of like a family."

"We ain't never had the money before," calls back Daryl Hence, turning away from a grill and pointing a spatula in Sam's direction. As a coach, Daryl won a national championship for the Warriors, in the 95-pound division. Brian and Pete served on his staff. This season he's accepted a position off the field, as Sam's assistant in charge of football. "I'd cook every Saturday if we had the money," he says.

Two lines of boys in painfully new cleats kick up dust as they toss each other wobbly spirals. Coaches from every weight level shake hands with parents—mothers usually, a few fathers, a few grandparents—who stop by to introduce themselves or just to sample the food. The 110s think they've got a winning team this year. The 85s look uncertain. The 145s could go either way, depending on their attitude. Anthony Beasley, the new offensive co-ordinator of the 95-pounders, talks up a mother.

"We're going to be running the Vertical Stretch, from Georgia Southern University," he says. "Have you heard of it? It's the toughest system there is. No one at this level has ever seen anything like it. Every game we're going to have a script. There's going to be a no-huddle offense." The mother's eyes appear to be glazing over. Beasley continues to ramble. "We teach them college skills, the footwork, the ballhandling. These boys, they got no habits yet. That's the best part of being a coach. You can call the shots on their footwork, on the routes they run, everything."

When Beasley finally takes a breath, the mother turns toward the picnic table, claiming a sudden craving for potato salad. Beasley trails behind. "We've got videos for them to watch. And for you to watch too, so you can help them learn the system," he continues. "Our motto is 'If You Believe It You Can Achieve It.' You know, we're not just trying to teach football. We're trying to teach them about life. If there's an attitude adjustment needed, we go to something we call 'boot camp.' It's extra calisthenics and stuff. Like I said, the whole system is based on Georgia Southern."

Head coach Brian Johnson, who has been at the picnic for several hours already, slumps over the hood of a pickup truck parked near the picnic table. His arms spread from the right headlight to the windshield, his chin rests on the round bicep of his right arm. A plastic visor tints his face green, making him look sick. Standing beside him, a man dressed in an Oakland Raiders jersey wants to know how the 95s look this year.

Brian rotates his head on his arm so he can face his interrogator. All the preparation, all the work on his computers, all the planning with coaches Pete and Beasley—it all seems to have gotten to him. Two days before the first practice Brian looks more tired than excited.

"Man, I don't know, you know?" he declares, adding a slow chuckle. "I got a system down. I got an offense and a defensive plan. We got good coaches. But as of right now, until I see the players we got, we just don't know."

Brian lifts his head off his arm. Over at the picnic table players of all ages and weights dive into the pile of free food. Diamond Pless manhandles a rack of ribs, his favorite meal. Coach Pete reaches for an ear of corn. Daryl flips more hamburgers, his face obscured by a curtain of smoke.

As the sun starts its slow summer descent into the Everglades, Sam Johnson, the Warriors' founder and main administrator, asks one of the boys to retrieve the yellow registration sign. The boy dutifully runs across the street and over to the sandwich board. Appraising its girth for a few seconds, he stretches his arms just wide enough to grab the sign on both sides. He struggles with its weight, stopping every few feet to rest and to regrip the plywood. Eventually, finally, he staggers over to the trailer that serves as the Warriors' temporary office. He locks the sign inside a storage shed, where it will wait out another year. Registration is over. The 2001 season of the Greater Miami Pop Warner football league is under way.

Chapter 1

First Practice

A silver Honda with opaque windows rolls to a stop in a parking lot at Hadley Park. The car's trunk pops open as a small boy climbs out the passenger-side door. The boy pulls out a new pair of cleats from the trunk. Holding the footwear in his small hands, he breaks into a sprint. His legs carry him across the jogging path, past a woman power-walking around a paved path, over to the playing field where the 95-pound Liberty City Warriors warm up.

Each weight division at Hadley Park occupies its own plot of practice field. The 110s stretch over by the game-day gridiron, which is never used for practice. The 145s run wind sprints near the tennis courts. The 95s own turf along the chain-link outfield fence of a baseball field. Coach Beasley, the offensive coordinator, has tied a yellow-and-black banner to the fence: "Believe it!!! Achieve it!!! 95 lb. Warriors."

Head coach Brian Johnson stands in the middle of the field, which is composed largely of dirt as fine and dry as cocoa powder. A black Nike floppy hat protects Brian's head from the 90-degree sun. Prescription sunglasses tint his eyes blue. Sweat trickles down his face, soaking his T-shirt and dotting one of the six pairs of Nike sneakers he owns. He's trying to look imposing, like a leader, but as he watches the boys run a lap around the park he starts to smile. He's been waiting for this day.

When Brian arrived at the field two hours ago, he brought props. Off-season runs to the Home Depot netted him yards of PVC pipe, elbow joints, glue, and a hacksaw, all of which he used to assemble an obstacle course of impressive complexity. Ten yards of rope netting wait to be skipped. A limbo bar hovering three feet above the grass needs to be ducked under. A dozen orange cones form a zigzag for the players to slalom through as if skiing.

During the day Brian delivers bolts, screws, and other machine parts to warehouses around Miami. Today he took the day off and loaded his work van with the obstacle course and the cones. Beasley cashed in a vacation day too. Coach Pete, who also skipped work, stands near a concrete light post, chilling in the narrow beam of shade the post provides. The brim of his black Liberty City baseball visor is pulled so low he has to crane his neck to make eye contact with the three other assistants as they roll in.

All the coaches, like all the players, are black. Coach Ed is a towering scarecrow with long, thin teeth stained by cigarettes. He'll oversee the offensive line. Lanky Coach Chico will assist Coach Pete, who is his girlfriend's father. Coach Tubbs has the cornerbacks. During the day Tubbs mows grass for the City of Miami Beach, his eyes blind to the tourists on Ocean Drive, his mower a monotonous whir as he daydreams about his evenings at Hadley Park.

"I just love football" Tubbs says after he slaps skin with Pete and Brian. "I was too short to play, you know, so I coach."

The first boys arrive back from their laps, breathing heavily. Sweat drips down smooth faces all frozen and serious.

"Run all the way in. Put your hands on your head. Run it all the way in. Everywhere we go we run," says Coach Ed. "Got to get in shape to play football. Ninety-five-pound football."

The boys stand in the line of shade from the light post, resting their hands atop their heads as they cool down. No one wears helmets or pads this first day. Instead they wear shorts and cleats or maybe tennis shoes as oversized as pontoon boats. Most have pulled their T-shirts up to their armpits to cool their lean stomachs. They are skinny, and tiny. The description "pencil neck" is more accurate than it is insulting. Brian's eleven-year-old daughter, Sha-nise, sprays water into the boys' open mouths.

"Boot camp" is what Brian calls the first week of practice. Every day for five straight days the routine is the same. After stretching in a lazy semicircle the boys run wind sprints, then crabs, which entail scurrying twenty yards backward on their hands and feet. At the PVC-pipe obstacle course they run through the netting, trying not to trip. Speed is deemphasized.

"Boy, once you get good at it then you can go fast. It's not about going fast. Take your time," Coach Chico counsels a player entangled in rope. "Run with your head up." The boys who trip run the drill again. There is no yelling. Some kids show superior form or surprising speed—"good hands and good hops," as Tubbs says.

"Head up," says Beasley to a boy watching his feet navigate the netting. "You've got to see that linebacker coming at you. Good job, little man."

After an hour of conditioning, the Warriors break into groups. Assistant coach Chico schools the linebackers on the proper three-point stance: feet behind the buttocks, chest parallel to the ground, right hand touching the turf for balance.

"You've got to get used to the cadence," Chico yells. He blows into a silver whistle. "Ready!" The linebackers drop into a squat. "Set!" They lean onto their fingers. "Hike!" Each boy explodes forward, running a few feet before stopping with awkward expressions. Do we stop here? Do we keep going? Coach Chico asks them to wrap their hands around his waist as if he were an oncoming ball carrier. He's not asking for tackles, or for the boys to use force. Still, Chico is six-foot-one and 205 pounds. The thought of tackling him—most of the boys can hope only to wrap themselves around one of his thighs—reduces them to giggles.

"Get mean!" barks Coach Pete in his Army drill instructor voice. "Wipe that smile off your face. Get ready to hurt somebody. Get mean! Come on, get mean!"

Ten feet away, Coach Beasley introduces the offense to the different positions in his complicated Georgia Southern system. Five

3

boys form an offensive line. Antwane, the probable quarterback, stands behind them. When asked to stare at the butt cheeks of the players in front of him, Antwane turns toward a teammate and giggles.

"He said butt cheeks!"

*   *   *

In 1929, store owners in Philadelphia banded to solve a common problem: "Teenagers with nothing to do were causing them great losses in acts of violence," according to Pop Warner league history. The founder of the league, Joseph Tomlin, was an ambitious stockbrocker whose job prospects on Wall Street were crippled by the Great Depression.

Although the game took off in Pennsylvania, selling youth football to America proved a challenge. Parents feared their boys would be injured playing such a violent sport.

"Articles published by doctors, educators and others [stated] that the game should be outlawed," according to the official history. At a symposium on sports for youth, held in 1953 and attended by delegates from the AMA, the American Academy of Pediatrics, and others, Tomlin called for professional support of youth football teams. "His presentation is interrupted by boos. At the close of the conference, a vote is taken for a ban on 'kid football' and is supported 43–1. Tomlin being the lone dissenting vote."

Tomlin was not deterred. He continued brainstorming ways to promote his unwanted sport. One of his friends suggested what became the first-ever "Kiddie Bowl," played in a snowstorm in front of 2,000 spectators. A team backed by a Philadelphia restaurant faced off against a team from New York, Sinatra's Cyclones, sponsored by the singer. The game became an annual tradition. Within a decade, the league grew from a thousand teams nationwide to more than twice that number. Forty years later, the number of teams has tripled. Pop Warner is the largest football league in America.

For all its growth—especially in the last decade—Pop Warner remains a somewhat disorganized operation. There are no Pop

Warner leagues in football-crazy Ohio, for instance. The national office takes great pains to point out Pop Warner's emphasis on scholastics, from the recognition of academic all-Americans to the awarding of college scholarships. Yet, for the 350,000 kids in Pop Warner, only $30,000 in scholarships are awarded annually.

Even in Miami, rival leagues vie for youth football talent. But Pop Warner is the only league that offers the possibility of playing for a national championship at Disney World. For that reason, Pop Warner is far and away Miami's dominant youth football league, home to the best players and the toughest competition.

*   *   *

There are a few moments in every football game when the crowd, the coaches, the cheerleaders . . . well, the cheerleaders are often flying in their own universe, completely uninterested in the play on the field—but everyone else, from the stands on down to the water boys and even to the players on the field, sees the collision coming and draws in a collective breath to be released on the moment of impact.

"FOOM!" A short word said quickly, exploded. It's supposed to begin with the letter B, but in the slow-motion anticipation of the crash, in the trigonometry of a defender and a running back vectoring toward each other, some air escapes prematurely. Everyone says it the same. And just about everyone says it. If the hit is especially brutal a coda of cackles will be tacked on. "Ha-ha! Look at his sorry, flattened, ball-carrying ass. That dude be laid out for real."

For the 95-pound Warriors the first "FOOM!" of the year comes at the first practice in full pads. The four-year-old super pee wees receive their equipment first. No one younger than age six is technically allowed to play Pop Warner. Interest in football in Liberty City, though, is so strong that the Warriors field a team of boys as young as age three. The super pee wees play eight games of full-contact tackle football against other black parks. The little boys pull heavy helmets onto their heads, causing a few players to topple over. Hands poke out from the pads like feelers on a lobster. At their level, where shoulder pads make it impossible for receivers to close their arms together, pass plays generally do not work. Not that anyone minds.

"When they out here they can't do no wrong," says one father as he watches his son struggle to dress.

The 95-pound Warriors try on their helmets for fit, selecting face-mask styles appropriate for the positions they will be playing.

"I play running back," says a chipmunk-cheeked boy named Brandon. "Give me the lumberjack helmet. I don't want a duck. I don't want to quack-quack. That's the kind of face mask where it goes way out here." He holds his hand six inches from his face and down below his collarbone. "A duck is the kind of face mask worn by linebackers."

It takes a while to adjust to the new pads. Diamond spits out his yellow mouthpiece during a lap around the practice field, earning him extra crabs when he returns to the light post. Others boys pull off their helmets for the run, another violation of policy, though one they were allowed just a weight class ago, at the 85s. After laps and crabs, the Warriors execute forty jumping jacks. Brian then asks everyone to lean to the right and touch their toes.

"Whoa, whoa, whoa!" snaps Brian. "Everybody know their right from their left, right? Right?" The Warriors drop to the dirt for leg lifts. Brian tells them to make some noise if it hurts. In response, when they lift their cleats off the ground, the boys pound their chests and warble Tarzan arias. First only Diamond, then also a defender named Stevie. Soon enough it's a movement that makes the practice field sound like the Amazon jungle.

"How do you feel?" barks Brian.

"Feel good!" the Warriors respond.

In truth, only a few boys feel good, for the first day in full uniform brings more than helmets and bulky padding. It brings a tradition some of the boys love, and most of the boys fear with such intensity they've cried through the wind sprints and jumping jacks. Full equipment means full contact.

"When the pads come on we like to say it's when the pit bulls become poodles," assistant coach Chico explains as he lines up the team for the Hamburger Drill. A crowd of more than fifty people gathers at the 95-pound practice site. Six teenagers on bicycles lean over their handlebars, their eyes aglow. Parents of boys in other weight classes wander over in search of a violent tackle.

"Whenever somebody do something like the Hamburgerin' Drill they get, like, a lot of people around here who quit watching they own children and they all watch the drill," says Sha-nise, coach Brian's daughter. "They just want to see somebody get hurt. This is the thing that shows how hard they [the player] is, how soft or how big they heart is."

In the Hamburger Drill, two boys enter what is effectively a gladiator pit. Each lies on their back about seven yards apart. One boy has a ball. When Brian calls out "Go!" both boys flip over, leap up, and run straight into each other. The boy without the ball tries to tackle the runner. The runner does not try to avoid the would-be tackler; instead he tries to knock him over. Preferably, he'd like to knock him unconscious, which is what happens to a timid young tackler named Arlis on the initial round of the drill.

This is Arlis's first year in football, and his first time running the drill. He's asked to tackle Brandon, the running back who asked for a lumberjack face mask. But Arlis has never worn football equipment before, much less tried to tackle anybody. When he faces the experienced Brandon, Arlis stands up too straight, exposing his soft solar plexus.

"FOOM!" The crowd howls as Brandon spears Arlis in the gut. Arlis falls to the ground.

"That! Is! How! You! Run! The! Ball!" Coach Chico cackles. "Show 'em you ain't scared!"

"Stand up, brother," exhorts Ed, Arlis's coach on the offensive line. "You better learn to stay low. Otherwise they gonna bust you up in the stomach like that. You gonna get hurt." Two boys grab Arlis's arms and stand him unsteadily in the horseshoe of spectators. Over his shoulder pads he wears a baggy white T-shirt decorated with Warner Bros. cartoon characters like Bugs Bunny, Marvin the Martian, and Road Runner. Porky Pig announces, "That's all, folks!"

"Some of the boys, they can't wait to put on the pads. They want to hurt someone. They got anger," says Sha-nise. "Phillip, that running back over there, he's got anger. Brandon, he got anger. Some out here, they think they hard but when they get in there they get scared. They talk tough, then they afraid to hit."

Sha-nise turns her attention back to the horseshoe. Phillip, the running back with anger, flattens his would-be tackler to an approving "FOOM!"

"But most of the boys around here," she adds, "they pretty tough."

Chapter 2

Liberty City

Judging by the brochures, Miami starts on South Beach. Art Deco masterpieces squat low and livable, a pastel fantasyland worthy of Disney. Condos outside the Deco district fight for sky space, each tower crowded with trust-funded club kids, Argentineans riding out economic collapse, and more than a few Americans starting their second act, burning bright and living way, way beyond their means. South Beach is nightclubs and movie shoots and New Yorkers broiling away a vacation on a beach of wide white sand.

The causeway points west. Past million-dollar yachts moored in the marina, past private isles colonized by Gloria Estefan, Rosie O'Donnell, and Cristina Saralegui, Cuban Miami's answer to Oprah Winfrey. Past Fisher Island, the wealthiest neighborhood in America, an enclave so exclusive (and paranoid) it's reachable only by ferry. Fisher Island is where Bill Clinton liked to stay when he was president, mingling among professional athletes and liquor barons and even, for a while, Oprah herself.

Downtown the skyscrapers ring Bayfront Park, a sweaty stretch of grass over which the fireworks explode every Independence Day. On New Year's Eve a sunglass-wearing tangerine climbs the façade of the Hotel InterContinental, marking the passage of time for fans from Norman, Oklahoma, or South Bend, Indiana, or whatever college town has relocated for the Orange Bowl football game. A drawbridge spans the mouth of the Miami River, where Tequesta Indians deterred Spanish explorers with a display of severed heads.

To the south gleams Brickell Avenue and its glass offices for lawyers and bankers profiting from foreign investment, much of it dirty. To keep going is to pass condos on Biscayne Bay, the shopping mall that is Coconut Grove, and eventually Coral Gables, with its stylish homes and Draconian zoning code. Hugging the shoreline, protected behind guard gates and high concrete walls, mansions flaunt wealth exponentially out of place in Miami proper, the poorest big city in America.

Drink in that poverty, north, in Little Havana. Cross Calle Ocho, clogged every March with more than a million people munching *tasajo* while listening to Elvis Crespo and Thalia perform on competing stages. Up seven blocks looms the Orange Bowl. On football Saturdays, University of Miami tailgaters stagger past vendors shouting, "*Arepa! Arepa! Arepa!*" to advertise snacks of mozzarella cheese melted between cornmeal pancakes. The rickety steel stadium sways with a crowd of sweating, dependably drunk fans, almost none of whom attended the expensive private school. These adopted Hurricanes collapse in ecstasy when archrival Florida State shanks a field goal to ensure another home win.

Continue up and over another bridge. Steer close to the spaghetti junction of expressways that dissects Overtown, destroying a vibrant neighborhood once considered the Harlem of the South. Drive past Jackson Hospital, where Army medics come for trauma training. Past the criminal court building and the county jail and the state attorney's office, where Janet Reno used to work.

Stay north, beyond the produce warehouses, onto Northwest 39th Street, the main artery of Allapattah. Once rich farmland, Allapattah now grows crops of used car lots, junkyards, and auto body shops. The storefronts advertise only in Spanish. A public high school cowers behind black iron bars sharpened at the tips. Mobile nightclubs with thumping salsa music and windows tinted absolute black cruise west past the jai alai fronton, past the airport, into the chaos that is Hialeah, the true Little Havana now that Calle Ocho is mostly Nicaraguan and Honduran.

Join a different parade. One not populated with the Lamborghinis seen on the Beach, nor the Mercedes from the Gables. Tricked-out Honda Accords lead a procession of lone-wolf sedans, wobbly in the wheels, uninsured without question, and piloted by refugees so persecuted in Haiti they never learned to read Creole, much less English. Follow these cars under the concrete pylons of the Dolphin Expressway into Liberty City. Travel where the tourists are specifically told, in no uncertain terms, to never, ever go.

Seventh Avenue is the main street, running parallel to I-95. The shops, mostly, are businesses in name only. Yes, there is a Burger King and a Walgreen's and a brave branch of the Washington Mutual Bank. The rest? Empty storefronts interrupted occasionally by the Jesus Miracle Center, or a blood bank, or Mr. Mohammad's Dry Cleaning and Mosque.

Liberty City is, in the words of one Warriors coach, a neighborhood "trending downward." The hub of race riots in the eighties and of dozens of gang-related assassinations in the nineties. The neighborhood where a German tourist who asked for directions was robbed, stabbed, and run over by her murderers. Yet most people raised in Liberty City defend their home with vicious pride. It's not only tolerable—in a way, it's even beautiful.

"There ain't no place like it," says Luther Campbell, the former front man of the rap group 2 Live Crew. "I mean, you know, Liberty City is the crown jewel of the whole entire South. If you go anywhere—if you go to Charlotte, if you go to Atlanta—you say you from Liberty City, you get the highest respect. I'm serious. You get the utmost respect because so many cats from Liberty City went out and passed the word, you know what I'm saying? Either being in sports or in music or being gangsters or being whatever. Liberty City—I mean, there ain't nothing like it."

* * *

September 22, 1951, 2:15 in the morning: the precise moment when two 100-pound sticks of dynamite exploded. The dynamite had been planted in an unoccupied building in Carver Village, a housing development originally named Knight Manor and built expressly as whites-only housing. Now, with a new name and with blacks moving in, Carver Village became the focal point of young Miami's fierce racial tensions.

The explosion ripped the roof off the building and tore doors and windows from their frames. Damage exceeded $200,000. Eight days later another early-morning bomb destroyed two more units at the housing project. Three more bombs exploded on December 2.

City leaders had inadvertently lit the fuse fifty-five years earlier, upon the founding of Miami. In the days before air-conditioning and before engineers learned how to tame the Everglades, South Florida was one large, hot, buggy swamp. The first blacks arrived at the turn of the twentieth century to clear roadways of palmetto trees and shrub roots, to build stores and a courthouse and the infrastructure of the new city. "As the City of Miami came to life, blacks living on the bay had no political power, recognition, or influence," writes historian Marvin Dunn. Yet at the incorporation of the city, in 1896, nearly half the voters were black. A black man was the first to sign the city's charter.

Many of these black pioneers were Bahamians who'd escaped economic disaster on their island. Although they were referred to as gentlemen at home, in Miami they found themselves living in strict segregation in an overcrowded settlement called Nigger Town. Blacks survived without electricity, running water, or indoor plumbing, though these amenities were common in white areas. Nigger Town became a breeding ground for tuberculosis and other diseases.

Conditions worsened when even more blacks arrived from Georgia and north Florida. Miami's balmy weather during the deep freeze of 1895 created a need for field workers, and prompted Henry Flagler to extended his railroad south from Palm Beach. Flagler's mostly black workforce joined the growing crowd in Nigger Town. Housing prices for blacks skyrocketed.

In the thirties, a visionary (and shrewd) white real estate man named Floyd Davis devised a solution to the problem. Davis, through

12

his attorney, proposed the construction of Liberty Square, which would be the largest housing project in the South, and, as he saw it, the nucleus of a new black settlement. Not only would Liberty Square relieve the housing crunch in Nigger Town, it would also make Davis a wealthy man; he owned much of the land on which the proposed complex would be built.

The project was a winner, for Davis and for the city. Blacks flocked to what was described as the most beautiful housing project in Florida. The thirty-four new homes featured hot water, electricity, and gas. Every family received a plot of land for a garden. Yet, as nice as the amenities were, the homes were still located in the Deep South: A six-foot-high-stone wall ringed the subdivision in which Liberty Square was built, a not-very-subtle reminder to blacks who might otherwise visit the surrounding white neighborhoods.

The success of Davis's vision prompted two more developers to cash in on the building boom by constructing their own black housing project inside the wall. At the same time, the pair erected a sister project just outside the wall and named it Knight Manor. The black project, as predicted, quickly filled. Knight Manor didn't fare so well; white renters leery of living so close to blacks never occupied more than half the complex.

In 1951, the two developers altered their bottom line, and Miami history, when they decided to rent 215 empty Knight Manor apartments to blacks. It was the first time in the history of super-segregated Miami proper that blacks were invited to live outside their clearly defined borders.

The plan met with fierce opposition. White citizens mobilized into groups with names such as the Dade County Property Owners Association and the John B. Gordon chapter of the Ku Klux Klan. White residents of Knight Manor held an "Indignation Meeting," followed by a motorcade in which they drove around the now-integrated project flashing their headlights. Some of the more law-abiding Klansmen obeyed a county ordinance banning cross burnings and instead ignited giant wooden Ks.

13

The burnings, and the subsequent bombings, did not prevent blacks from moving to Knight Manor in growing numbers. So strong was the demand for affordable housing that the boundaries of the black neighborhood soon stretched beyond Knight Manor to encompass the larger section of Miami that is now known as Liberty City.

❧ ❧ ❧

"To the rest of the world looking in, they probably would say that in looking at Liberty City it's almost like they're looking at a Monet or the *Mona Lisa*," says Luther Campbell. "It's just a city within itself, man. It's like, there's so much we done work through here. I mean, from poverty to the riots to the gang wars in the nineties and the dope and all that. I mean, even when you look at the bad things, like the riots, you see a community coming together to try to fight whatever it may be, oppression or whatever."

Campbell is standing in Gwen Cherry Park, the home field of Pop Warner's successful Bulls program. He is wearing a white Miami Hurricanes visor, white Hurricanes shorts, and a sleeveless white Miami Hurricanes T-shirt. A tattoo on his right shoulder advertises Luke Records, the company for which he earned his renown. 2 Live Crew's 1990 album, *As Nasty As They Wanna Be*, featured a single, "Me So Horny," which sampled the solicitation of a Vietnamese prostitute in a Stanley Kubrick movie. When a Broward County judge declared the album obscene after adding up eighty-seven references to oral sex, Campbell and his crew received attention far beyond what was due such relative unknowns. Appeals of the ruling climbed all the way to the U.S. Supreme Court, where Campbell emerged victorious. Thanks to the controversy, sales of *As Nasty As They Wanna Be* reached double platinum.

"Sex sells" is a maxim Campbell has capitalized on ever since. His stated goal is to become the black Hugh Hefner. To that end, his unclelukesworld.com is a portal to raw black sex, featuring a "Freak Show pay-per-view," "Luke's eye candy" of "exotic pix from girls around the world," and "Luke's XXX Files." A live sex show broadcast offers "24 hours of non-stop freaking! Tell them what to do and they'll do it!" Although his days in 2 Live Crew are long behind him, Campbell remains a player in the music business. In 1999 he returned to the *Billboard* charts with his single "Lizard Lizard."

Despite the raunchiness of his public image, Campbell is known as much in Liberty City for his philanthropy as for his music. He sponsors an annual Easter egg hunt for neighborhood kids. He hosts charity golf tournaments. And he, more than anyone else, is responsible for the revival of Pop Warner football, not just in Liberty City but in all of black Miami.

Football eclipses music as Campbell's great passion. He attended neither Northwestern High nor Jackson High, yet when those schools meet in the Soul Bowl, Campbell watches the game standing on the field. He enjoyed field privileges at every UM home game as well, until it was discovered he was paying bounties of $100 or more to Hurricanes who leveled particularly hard hits on the other teams' star players.

"In Miami you got to play football," he says. "If you're a kid, I mean, the first thing is, like you have to play football in order to even have any kind of man in you. It's serious. It's almost like football is like becoming a man, it's a whole part of showing that you are tough. And in Miami, to be honest with you, it's mostly blacks that play the game. Baseball in Miami is predominantly Latin. And football is predominantly black."

When Campbell was coming up in Liberty City there were no youth football leagues in his neighborhood. He and his friends traveled by bus nine miles every day to Miami Beach to practice and play for a program in that city's Flamingo Park. He continued traveling to Miami Beach to attend high school and to play cornerback for the Beach Hi-Tides, a fairly mediocre team. But even transplanted outside his neighborhood, Campbell and his friends stayed true to their roots.

"I'm all about community," he says. "And in the time I was growing up that's what we was lacking. The only thing we had was the pride that we came from Liberty City, you know what I'm saying? And we could kick anybody's ass outside Liberty City, and that was for real. We felt that we was tougher, harder than anyone, and any other team we'd go out and play we wouldn't really be representing the team—we'd be representing Liberty City.

"I always said if I get a couple of cents to my name over my lunch money I'm going to try and start a program in Liberty City. And the first thing I was going to do was make sure none of those players had to travel to practice on no bus."

As soon as 2 Live Crew stumbled upon success, Campbell began building youth football. He found a Miami police officer interested in starting a sports program. Together they teamed up with a third man, Sam Johnson, a bus driver who was running a modest after-school baseball league in Hadley Park. After Johnson agreed to launch a football team, Campbell donated significant seed money to the Liberty City Optimist Club. The Warriors were born.

In the organization's first year in Pop Warner football, the Warriors won city championships in seven of eight weight divisions. Liberty City's on-field success spawned sister programs in half a dozen more black parks: the Gwen Cherry Bulls, the Inner City Jaguars, the Overtown Rattlers, even the New Birth Saints, representing Miami's largest black church. Some of the programs are struggling start-ups; others, like Gwen Cherry, have already won national championships.

"A lot of people come to me asking to donate money," Campbell says. "But with this, I can come out here and see results."

Even with the expansion from Liberty Square, the black housing crunch never abated. White leaders continued to covet property in Overtown, the name by which Nigger Town came to be called. One white activist encouraged the wholesale relocation of Overtown's residents to vacant lots far north and west of downtown. Such grand social engineering proved unnecessary in the late sixties, when federal transportation officials steered the new I-95 expressway through Overtown's main business district.

"One massive highway interchange alone destroyed the housing of approximately ten thousand people," writes historian Raymond Mohl. "Despite official promises, few replacement housing units were built, and those people who were uprooted got little in the way of relocation assistance."

The housing supply was further strained by the arrival of thousands of Caribbean and Latin American immigrants, whose movement into the cheapest apartments available elsewhere kept Miami's blacks confined to sharply demarcated areas.

"Take the neighborhood where I grew up in Winston-Salem, North Carolina," offers T. Willard Fair, president of the Urban League of Greater Miami. "The blacks moved out into the cheap housing that was left in the white neighborhoods. In Miami those affordable houses are taken by the Haitians and the Cubans. The black people are trapped."

This shortage of affordable housing has been cited as a factor in every riot in modern Miami history, including the devastating 1980 outbreak that followed the acquittal of the police officers who killed insurance salesman Arthur McDuffie, a thirty-two-year-old black man who was clubbed to death with police flashlights after being pulled over for what amounted to a traffic infraction.

Thirteen people were killed in the riot that followed the acquittal of the officers by an all-white jury. As the sun set on the Saturday the verdict was announced, residents of Knight Manor pulled up lawn chairs to watch a mob of blacks murder five whites who innocently drove down 62nd Street. One driver, an eighteen-year-old warehouse worker returning from a day at the beach, was beaten, run over with his car, shot multiple times, stabbed with a screwdriver, and smashed in the skull with a yellow newspaper dispenser.

Outside the Scott Homes, the largest housing project in the state, rioters showered rocks onto a car driven by a fifty-five-year-old woman. When she hit the brakes, the rioters poured gas on her car and ignited it, burning her to death.

Nine years later, after another all-white jury acquitted yet another Miami cop in the killing of a black man, riots ravaged the same Scott Homes during the week the city hosted the Super Bowl. That's one reason why, when the Super Bowl returned to Miami in 1995, the NFL donated $1 million to build a recreation center in Gwen Cherry Park, in the center of the Scott projects.

"Look at this motherfucker," Campbell says, standing outside the rec center on a Saturday afternoon. The boxy structure has orange concrete walls, tinted glass, and a green metal roof. In addition to a 9,000-square-foot gym, the center features two computer labs and space for tutoring and art classes. The Miami Dolphins and other businesses covered the rest of the building's $3.1 million cost.

The 110-pound Gwen Cherry Bulls are playing a game in the park against an opponent from southern Miami-Dade. A half-dozen barbecue grills pump out a cloud of charcoal smoke and chicken fat that hovers over the main field like a misty blimp. Standing up in the fifth and highest row of bleachers, gits—local slang for gang members—puff on blunts while they berate the coaches.

"Y'all better start throwing the ball!"

Most of the players on the Bulls, and most of the thousand or so spectators, used to live in the Scott projects. The city recently condemned the projects and relocated the occupants. Decentralizing public housing is a popular concept implemented in St. Louis, Chicago, and several other cities. But when Campbell looks at the rows of boarded-up town houses ringing Gwen Cherry, he sees only blacks once again uprooted from their homes.

"This is probably the first building that has been built for blacks in God knows how many years and the fucking NFL had to come in and do a Super Bowl and put the building here," he says. "This park has been empty all our lives here, just like them projects is empty now. What they're going to do is end up making them into motherfucking condos or something, just like happened in Overtown. It's exactly the same. They'll take over that motherfucker and push all the black people out.

"What you keep doing is you keep disenfranchising people, keep on doing it, keep on doing it, keep on doing it. You keep moving 'em here, moving them there, eventually they move the fuck out. That's what this is all about here. This center that was built here, if you come back here in ten years there won't be any blacks using this building. This will probably be a Latin community."

On the field, a Bulls quarterback tosses a spiral into the hands of his wide receiver. Parents heckle the refs. Ice cream trucks blare competing jingles. The cloud of barbecue smoke floats over young boys licking snow cones drizzled in grape and cherry syrup.

"At the end of the day this might be the most therapeutic thing for us, this right here," Campbell says, surveying the field. "We be coming out here leaving our worries, our troubles, our problems with the election and how they fuck us over, how they rob us for our land and everything. We come out here and we focus on this here, playing football, camaraderie. That's the only thing we got. They can't take this shit from us."

He looks out at the football field for a full two minutes, saying nothing. Bulls players exchange hugs after scoring a touchdown. Coaches shout encouragement. Campbell glances at the rec center, then back at the field.

"That's what we own," he says finally. "We own this game. I mean, you can take whatever you want to take—our land, our housing, our jobs, whatever. But we got our dignity and our pride. We might not have ever had any leader to lead us to the promised land, but at least we got our football. We own football."

Chapter 3

Campos

F lorida City is a perfectly flat, scrap-poor outpost on the southern tip of the Continental United States. The town sits just north of the Florida Keys and just east of Everglades National Park. Revenue streams in primarily from the fast-food restaurants serving Key West–bound tourists, and from federal aid money still flowing a decade after Hurricane Andrew almost blew Florida City off the map. The football field is the main park in the city, and it, along with the concession stand that serves it, was improved with hurricane relief money. Cars park outside the field on a row of concrete slabs, souvenirs of the tent city erected for laborers displaced by the storm. At twilight, flat fields of green beans stretch beyond the cars to touch a horizon of fading purple light.

More than two thousand people—almost a quarter of the town's population—crowd the bleachers or stand on the sidelines. Their chests press against yellow boundary ropes protecting the playing field. Under halogen lights, in the heat of early September, a nightclub vibe infuses the park. Girls strut in clingy minidresses. Guys mack in baggy FUBU Platinum and white tank tops accessorized with thin ropes of gold. One man covers his tank in a heavy denim jacket, fashionable in New York maybe but dangerously hot in a tropical summer that is two months from breaking. The humidity is so stifling that, just before kickoff, a cheerleader faints from exhaustion and is dragged off the field by her shoulders.

Maybe all these people are here because in Florida City on a Saturday night there isn't much else to do. Certainly they've come out to support their Razorbacks as they battle in Pop Warner's heavyweight 145-pound division. The more probable reason for the turnout—and anyone here wearing a baby blue Razorbacks T-shirt and shaking a noisemaking plastic bottle filled with rocks will admit as much—is they're here to see the coach on the visitors' sideline. And they're hoping, frankly, that their Razorbacks kick him and his whole team right in the ass.

"Campos, you a punk!" shouts a Florida City booster as the Palmetto Raiders take the field for the opening kickoff.

"Your cracker ass ain't shit," taunts a man with a full bridge of gold teeth. "You're whole team ain't shit."

Raul Campos, the self-described greatest youth football coach who ever lived, is used to the venom. "Once you have established a dominating coaching form for a number of years, other coaches begin to fear you," the two-time national champion writes in his unpublished autobiography, "Winning It All." "It is as though they know that they have no hope in winning, no matter how good they might be. They really don't want to play you. As long as this weighs on the back of their minds, no matter what they say or do, they cannot beat you."

Campos and his assistant coaches patrol their sideline dressed, as always, as if attending a funeral: black slacks, black shoes, white dress shirts, and silky black ties. "You should always maintain a neat appearance," Campos advises in his autobiography. "When you look good, you feel good. When you feel good, you perform better. Take care in how you present yourself to the world."

Campos tops off his game-day outfit with a black Raiders cap pulled over a mop of hair the same silver as his beard. Even at night he continues to sport wraparound sunglasses so wide and dark they mask his fleshy face. Sweat soaks every inch of his oxford. A T-shirt now visible underneath advertises a typical Palmetto taunt: "Raider Nation: We Don't Rebuild, We Reload."

Only fifteen miles separate Florida City from Palmetto Field, where Campos's team practices and plays its home games. Rather than let his players catch rides from friends or coaches, Campos insists they arrive as a team, and in style. A chartered motor coach makes his players feel special, like they're part of a professional outfit. And he knows the way it plays with the heads of the Razorbacks when it rolls in. (The bus, nice as it is, is actually a step down for the Raiders. Two seasons ago Campos transported his players in rented Hummer limousines. He stopped that practice only when league officials protested.)

Playing with the heads of the opposing team is a Campos specialty. Every Pop Warner player must weigh no more than a certain amount, in the case of this year's Campos team, 145 pounds. Prior to the player weigh-ins that preceded the game, the coach ordered his team to psych out the Razorbacks.

"Whenever they line up for weigh-in, I want them to do one or two things, depending on the opponent," Campos notes in his autobiography. "One is to look right through them, and the other is not to look their way but to act as if the opponent does not exist. Either way, it is our way of telling them that we are going to be in their faces all afternoon or that their presence is so weak that we've decided to ignore them."

Florida City fumbles the opening kick and the Raiders recover. One play later, running back Carl Martin scores on a straightforward run up the middle. Florida City fumbles again, setting up a second Palmetto touchdown. One Razorback receiver, finding himself wide open downfield, drops a perfect pass rather than risk punishment from two oncoming Raider defenders. The crowd groans in disgust. Campos, under his hat, behind his dark glasses, relishes his opponents' pain. He's fucked with their heads. They're beating themselves.

"Come on, Palmetto, bust their ass!" shouts a woman in the stands as the score climbs to 20–0, Raiders. Not everyone, it should be noted, hates Palmetto's head coach. Standing along the rope behind the Raiders bench, Campos's supporters fan Razorback anger by waving a line of black-and-silver T-shirts:

"Big Ballers: Palmetto Raider Football," states one T-shirt.

"Raider Football: Best of the Best."

"Palmetto Raiders: Mercy Rule in Effect."

◆ ◆ ◆

Two days after crushing Florida City, Raul Campos leans on the edge of an overstuffed leather couch in a TV room just off his kitchen. Gloria, his second wife, sets a plate of beefsteak, black beans, and yellow rice on the countertop and tells him dinner is ready.

"Yeah, all right," he mumbles, not looking at her. The big-screen TV projects a grainy videotape of a high school game played somewhere in California. The tape is a few years old. It's been viewed so many times the colors of the players' uniforms have faded. To a certain stratum of hard-core football coaches scattered across America, the tape is regarded as a sacred text. One of the California teams featured on the videotape runs an offense that is unlike any system ever seen. Even after one watches a half hour of plays, with Campos using a remote control to forward and reverse and pause and slow-motion crucial moments, it's hard to describe what is happening on the field. All eleven players gather at the line of scrimmage in a tight huddle resembling a group hug. When the ball is snapped it's unclear who in the huddle gets the ball, and therefore whom the defense should tackle. This offense, Campos notes with amazement, scores a lot of points.

Campos belongs to three Internet coaching chat rooms. The members of each room collect and trade videotapes and playbooks from high school, college, and professional teams. Playbooks, which contain the DNA of a team's strategy, are usually guarded obsessively. Yet just last week "a friend" forwarded Campos a copy of the playbook with which the University of Oklahoma defeated Florida State in the most recent Orange Bowl.

"I win not because I'm great or anything like that," Campos clarifies while pressing a button to rewind the videotape, which he's watched more than fifty times. "I study the game. I have plays in notebooks from years ago. Other teams can't stay with us. It's like a grad student going against someone just coming out of high school. It's like a chess grand master playing someone who's looking at a chessboard for the first time in their lives."

Raul Campos was born in Cuba eight years before the revolution. He says that when Fidel Castro seized his family's construction business, his parents shipped him and his older sister to Miami. They were supposed to live with an aunt. The aunt's boyfriend, apparently, had other ideas, and ordered the kids out of the house. Campos's sister enrolled in a Catholic girls' school in Pennsylvania. Campos ended up in Miami, in the equivalent of a youth hall.

Campos offers no specifics on where this youth hall was located. He declined repeated requests to tour the site. What details he is willing to convey about his time there are included in his autobiography. Life, he writes, was difficult. He was forced to grow up quickly, to learn how to defend himself.

"I had earned respect but I didn't like what was happening to me," he explains in his memoirs. "I was becoming a thug, like all the other guys there. Every other word that came out of my mouth was a swear word. And what made it worse and what hurt me the most was that I was beginning to not care."

Campos credits football for turning around his wayward youth. Campos played baseball in Cuba, and considers himself to have been a good pitcher. It was in the youth hall that a coach introduced him to American football. The discipline he needed to excel at football helped him out in the classroom. His grades went up. His behavior improved. Eventually he landed a scholarship to the University of Florida, where he played on an offensive line that protected Heisman Trophy winner Steve Spurrier. At least that's what he says. No one at the university can confirm that Campos played for the Gators, or that he even attended the school.

"Football changed my life's perspective; it gave me something to live for again," he writes. "To this day I respect the game that saved me, educated me, and educated my two sons, one of whom plays in the National Football League. I'd probably be either dead or in prison if it weren't for football. That's why, when I'm asked what I am doing coaching kids, I simply respond: Because this is where I belong."

Campos lives in Country Walk, a middle-class subdivision southwest of Miami, near the zoo. Country Walk is a dense maze of similar-looking homes all connected with identical white plywood fences. Even after providing a visitor explicit directions to his house, Campos often must meet his guest at a convenience store and drive him the final mile. Security guards in golf carts patrol the development. Any cars parked on the street are towed immediately and without warning.

Like many subdivisions in western Miami-Dade County, Country Walk was built on the cheap. Contractors used shoddy materials and paid little attention to the county's hurricane-strict building code. Andrew's 100-mile-per-hour winds transformed Country Walk into a national symbol for slipshod construction. The development all but disappeared. Roofs blew off. Walls blew down. Entire houses collapsed like matchsticks.

Campos saw an opportunity. The hurricane had decimated his house too, out in the more rural Redlands neighborhood. Rather than rebuild that house—he works in the construction business, primarily supervising the building of new public schools—he purchased fifteen destroyed Country Walk homes, rebuilt all of them, and resold fourteen of them at what he says was a fantastic profit. The fifteenth home, upon his wife's insistence, he moved into.

A stuffed deer guards the front door, the only taxidermy saved from a menagerie of more than sixty trophies Campos says he owned before the hurricane. Upstairs, past the deer, is a loft hallway furnished with an overstuffed love seat, a table, a TV and VCR, and a bank of tapes on football strategy. The tapes have titles such as *The*

Bunch Attack, Coaching Fastbreak Football, and *Football's Split 4-4 Defense vs. the Run.* Included among the tapes is a copy of the 1996 Hula Bowl, in which Campos's son from his first marriage played as a linebacker for the University of Louisville. (That son proceeded to play professionally for the Dallas Cowboys and the Carolina Panthers.)

"I scout teams on Saturday or, if we're playing at the time, I have one of my assistant coaches scout for me," Campos says. "If I see the team we're about to play is running a certain kind of offense or defense, I can pull out a tape and see exactly what it's all about. I can see what formations to put up against it."

In addition to the videotapes, the shelves sag with dozens of playbooks Campos has obtained from friends. He owns a photocopy of the playbook the University of Michigan used in 1905 to run the pioneering single wing offense. He owns playbooks from smaller colleges such as Willamette and Wyoming and James Madison, schools that must innovate to counter the talent divide.

"I've got tapes of the University of Delaware's Winged T, which you've probably already heard of," he says, pointing to a tape in a black plastic box. "It was copied by schools all over. I have all the Dallas Cowboy playbooks from when my son played for them. I've got the Houston Gamblers from back in 1982 in the defunct USFL, back when they were instituting the run-and-shoot. The Denver Gold, also from the USFL, I got all their playbooks too."

Trophies overwhelm an end table next to the bookshelf. The 1999 Pop Warner national championship of the 110-pound pee wee division. The 2000 Pop Warner national championship of the 125-pound junior midget division. "Those are just some of the trophies," he says. "I've got dozens more in boxes in other rooms."

It's far from certain that Campos should clear shelf space for a third national championship trophy. The 2001 season is off to a bad start. Although the Raiders destroyed Florida City, the win came one week after a loss to Richmond, another predominantly black team that plays in a park near the southern leg of the Palmetto Expressway. Campos's loss, his first in three years, was unexpected. For him, it's flat-out unacceptable, maybe even incomprehensible.

In the two weeks since his defeat, Campos has assembled a box of paperwork that reveals, he insists, that the Richmond team is stocked with overage players, high school dropouts, and certified criminals. He learned most of this by illegally tapping into the county public school system computer database.

"I have full access to the schools, since I build them," he says. "I have access to the alarm systems. I have access to the computers. I go on there and compare. I have all the proof on paper."

*   *   *

Campos takes a seat at his dining room table, pushing aside a pile of playbooks, several sheets of paper upon which he's scribbled ideas for plays, and a copy of his autobiography, which he's still shopping around to publishers. He is wearing a blue T-shirt upon which is printed the words "Big Dog." His head is massive, maybe 20 percent larger than the head of an average man. His face is full and fleshy. His thick fingers struggle to extract a piece of paper from a folder of all his players.

"The essential part of my offense is speed," he notes. "And that's something I've got a lot of. My wide receivers are lethal. My runners are awesome. Even if blitzing, the other team's linebackers can't catch my quarterback."

Speed, of course, can be viewed as a euphemism. His lethal wide receivers, runners, and quarterback are all black. If he were to build his offense around the suburban boys who live closest to Palmetto Field, there's little chance he'd be scoring so many touchdowns, or winning so many championships.

Prior to his success at Palmetto the past two seasons, Campos coached for a few years at rival Goulds Park. When Campos returned to Palmetto Field he inherited a team comprised of sorry suburban boys, the losers of every game. He addresses the subsequent turnaround in his autobiography:

"I could hardly believe it. There I was at the 50-yard line of the Disney Sports Center, being presented with the United States

National Youth Football Championship trophy. As I stood there, my mind wandered back to how it had all started, and how we had come to win the most coveted prize of United States youth football—the Pop Warner Super Bowl. It felt like a dream come true, as if I had won the real Super Bowl.

"How was it possible that a team that had not won a single game during the previous year had turned it around and won a national championship?"

Over the course of the next 150 pages, Campos makes it perfectly clear how he achieved the turnaround. He scouted his opponents and plotted his game plans thoroughly. He taught players to believe in themselves, drilling them constantly on such fundamentals as a good fake or a good sidestep. He instituted a dress code to foster pride in appearance. And, mentioned almost as an afterthought, he cut *every single player* from the team that lost all its games and replaced them with blue-chip studs from West Perrine.

To attract such speedy talent, Campos must make his program appealing. There are the rides in the deluxe motor coach, the on-field oxygen tank, the steak dinners he pays for after games, and the varsity letter jackets to wear to the restaurant. He also dangles the grand prize: a promise of a winning season, a city championship, and a week's vacation in Disney World, all expenses paid.

Yet even with such incentives to play for the Raiders, he must defend his roster against poachers from other teams. Campos flips through his roster to illustrate the fluid nature of Pop Warner allegiances. He stops on the page with the name and emergency contact information for Jarmaine Brockington, a lithe boy with dreadlocked hair, an engaging smile, and the prestigious title of half-brother of Trick Daddy, successor to Luther Campbell as the most popular rapper in Miami. Trick Daddy's sophomore album, *Thug.com*, cracked the *Billboard* top ten.

"That kid, it's hard to get him to concentrate," Campos admits, referring to Jarmaine. "When he goes home he's exposed to orgies and drugs and all the vices of adulthood. How you going to get him to concentrate on football?"

Whatever his concentration level, Jarmaine is an unquestionably gifted athlete. He started at running back last year on Suniland's national championship team. When the league suspended Suniland's coach for running up the score in the national championship game, Jarmaine shopped around for another park with the best odds of one, showcasing him, and two, getting him back to Disney World. He first went to play for the Richmond Giants. Somehow he was convinced to transfer his allegiance to Palmetto.

"Hey, I've lost kids of my own," Campos counters. "I've either had to cut 'em or they've asked for transfers. If a kid wants to go, we give 'em the release. I don't care. If they don't want to be with us I don't want 'em."

Tommy Hoffman, the quarterback of Suniland's championship team, transferred to Palmetto as well. In the first game of the season, Campos placed Hoffman on the offensive line, the least glamorous position there is. Hoffman quit the Raiders the next day. Hoffman was expendable because Campos's Raiders are loaded with talent.

"There's Kenny Henry—he's a wide receiver," Campos says, returning to his roster. "Randall Henry is his actual name. This is his first year playing for us. He's a very good receiver, very fast."

Randall Henry earned all Fs and one B in his last grading period. He's eligible to play for the Raiders only because his guidance counselor signed a waiver. Why is Campos playing such a bad student? And by playing such a bad student, what differentiates his program from Richmond's supposedly rogue program?

"If I don't do it, he'll just end up playing for someone else," Campos says, flipping pages to locate some of his other studs: Xavier Thomas, the fastest kid on the team; Bryan Revere, Campos's quarterback for the past four years, first at Goulds and now at Palmetto; and Eric Moore, who's slow in practice but "like butter" in games.

"Carl Martin is number five, a big running back," Campos continues. "He's been with me for four years, meaning he came up with us when we moved up from Goulds. He's probably the best running back in the whole league."

Campos flips to a last page of his binder. The data sheet refers to a teenager named Courtney Burns. On the videotape Campos produced to commemorate his back-to-back championships, Courtney Burns is all over the place. Courtney scoring a touchdown here, catching another touchdown there. A minute later, Courtney scoring again, long legs running away from defenders, speed so fast he embarrasses those trying to tackle him.

"He's been with us for two years," Campos says. "He's the main reason why we won nationals. He was a super-good runner." Campos pushes up his bifocals, which have slipped down the bridge of his nose. Then he folds his hands over Courtney's bio page.

"He hasn't run much for us this year, though," he says of Courtney. "He's not running as good, I don't know why. Kids are like that—different from one year to the next. Especially at this age, where there are a lot of distractions. In his case, his brother was shot and killed in the off-season; that could be disturbing him a lot. His concentration is not there like it was last year."

Campos stopped giving Courtney the ball in games, which prompted Courtney to briefly quit. He came back a week later and asked to rejoin the team. Campos put the matter up for a vote. The other players elected to reinstate him. Campos didn't care one way or another.

"If they wouldn't have taken him back I would have been fine with it," Campos reveals. He closes the binder. "Like I said, for whatever reason he's simply not running the ball too good."

Chapter 4

Diamond

Georgia Southern University's football team runs something called the Horizontal and Vertical Stretch offense. With this scheme, the Eagles have won six national championships at the Division I-AA level. In 1997, Georgia Southern's offense averaged a phenomenal 419 passing yards—and 50 points—per game. The Horizontal and Vertical Stretch has been called the most difficult offensive system in football, at any level. Georgia Southern students spend months studying their playbooks before ever setting foot on a practice field. The Liberty City Warriors, some of whom are only eight years old, are still learning their multiplication tables. Nevertheless, the Horizontal and Vertical Stretch is the cornerstone of the Warriors' offense this year.

"It's shaping up," reports Coach Beasley, the assistant installing the Georgia Southern system. "I expect our quarterback to score on the first play of the year. The kid who plays defense against him isn't going to know what to do. They've never seen a system like ours."

Neither have any of the Warriors. After nearly a month of drills, Antwane, the quarterback, remains dazzled by the complicated offense. To help him grasp his responsibilities on each snap Antwane wears a black armband the size of his forearm. On the band, color-coded in red, yellow, and green ink, is a diagram of all the plays he's supposed to know.

"34 Vere. That's three numbers, right?" Beasley asks Antwane, apparently rhetorically. "If I say 34 Vere, how should you call the play in the huddle? If I give you the number 2, the guy in the huddle will come in and say, 'Coach says run 21 Vere.' You know what that means, right?" Beasley scribbles some plays on a marker board as Antwane stares at him. "That means you go to the left side and fire a home run. That's the first play of our first game. Sedrick is the wideout. He's going to score a touchdown. They won't know what hit 'em."

Beasley has one more week to make sure everyone learns his role. Although it's September and the Warriors have been practicing since late July, the team has yet to play a game. Its first scheduled opponent, the Inner City Jaguars, failed to field a squad at the 95-pound level. The Warriors won by default.

A young woman in stiletto heels wobbles toward the practice area. She's wearing a tight denim miniskirt and a yellow cotton blouse, the top four buttons undone. Tattoos flash over her arms, shoulders, and cleavage. Her straight hair is pulled back in a ponytail to reveal a pair of malevolent eyeballs inked just above her neckline, new ammunition for a mother's classic threat of eyes in the back of her head.

Shakitha Wallace walks over to Coach Pete, who's gulping water near the concrete light post.

"He's a little behind," she says, speaking of her son, Diamond Pless. She says that he needs to be better coached than he was last year on the 85-pound team, that those fools weren't sharp enough to recognize Diamond's talent. Pete nods while swishing water between his cheeks.

"We don't coach here," he reassures her. "We teach them the game."

"That's why we here," she says, pulling a can of strawberry soda out of her purse. She leans back against the shady side of the concrete light post. Her key ring states, "I have PMS and a gun. Excuse me, do you have something to say?"

Diamond owns a pair of lucky green socks that he used to wear to football practice until he burned a hole in the right heel. Now he practices in black cotton socks with his name climbing down his shins in yellow felt letters. His practice jersey is an oversized white T-shirt with the word "GREAT" embossed on the front, an acronym for Gang Resistance Education and Training. The shirt drapes below Diamond's knees. He is 43 inches tall. Even among boys his young age he is short. Further hampering his Warrior image, his helmet sits back on his head, making it look like he is constantly scanning the sky for airplanes.

Diamond has asked to be a wide receiver. Actually, the request came from his mom, who is in negotiations with Brian and the other coaches. Her son, she insists, is blessed with innate, blazing speed. If the coaches are smart, she advises, they'll harness this speed. To ensure they do, Shakitha is a fixture at Warrior practices.

On the day of the first Hamburger Drill, when Diamond stepped into the pit for the first time, Shakitha pushed her way to the front of the crowd, taking a position two feet from her son. "All right, Diamond!" she cheered when he eluded a tackle. On the next play he earned a good gain before being wrapped up by a tackler. "Keep those legs movin'! Keep those legs movin'!" Shakitha shouted. When Diamond rotated out of the drill, she patted him on the helmet. "Legs moving. No matter what, got to keep you legs moving."

"She tough on him," Brian's daughter Sha-nise says of the relationship between Diamond and his mother. "He can't get in a word. She thinks he run fast—real fast—but to me he don't."

Brian calls for a series of plays featuring long passes. Diamond, lined up in the slot, or wide receiver position, is instructed to sprint fifteen yards, turn around, and make a catch. When Diamond runs he doesn't move his arms. While the rest of his body bounces and rattles downfield, his thin limbs are cocked at the elbows like prongs on a forklift. As the ball he is supposed to catch spirals through the air, Diamond circles near its landing area, never bringing his hands together. The ball smacks the ground untouched, incomplete.

"Somehow we're going to find a way to get your momma a playbook," Beasley says, pulling Diamond aside. "You're going to take that home and you're going to study it. You flip the first page and that's our running plays. You flip the next page and that's our pass routes. It's all there. Gotta get this down, Diamond. Right now you lost."

Coach Brian joins in: "You know why you ain't getting it?" he asks, bending over to stare into Diamond's face. "'Cause you're zonin'." Diamond's expression is blank, as if he's tuning out. His helmet remains angled toward the clouds.

"Bro, this is conventional," Brian snarls. "All you gotta do is stay focused. Understand me?"

◆ ◆ ◆

Diamond attends Santa Clara Elementary School, in Liberty City. Most of his Warrior teammates attend the same school. He doesn't get the best marks. Before he made it to fourth grade he considered himself a math wizard. Then came long division. Now he pulls down Cs in math, the same grade he earns in English class, and in Spanish. His one A is in art.

"I'm good at art," he says. "I paint pictures. I draw pictures. I do a lot of stuff. We make posters and cards, like, for the holidays, and we watch art tapes. We do a lot of stuff. And we make all these little glass things. Today I made, like, this heart. It was this clay and for some reason the teacher she did some stuff to it and turned it into this hard kind of glass."

Diamond's enthusiasm for art class may be related to his passion for clothes. The closet in his room explodes with FUBU and Phat Farm. He prefers designer labels, and files specific requests when his mom goes shopping. His specialty is matching the right shirt with the right pair of pants.

Diamond shares the room with his younger sister, Artoria, age six. Sometimes, after 9 P.M., after they've both climbed into the lone bed and turned out the lights, he'll lie on his side atop the tan fitted sheet, unable to sleep. In the urban incandescence pouring through the room's plastic blinds, he can make out the art-class posters he's affixed to the walls. An easel holds a crinkly piece of paper on which he's scribbled the names of all fifty states and all but one of the corresponding state capitals. His sister's toys rest in a pile by the door, annoying Diamond's sense of decorum. "That's how the room be getting dirty!" Just outside the window cars zoom down I-95. The traffic flows so steady at night it's almost soothing. Not soothing enough, though, to lull him to sleep.

If he's watched professional wrestling on TV before bed he might fantasize that he's grappling with Triple H or the Undertaker. Maybe he'll spend a few minutes musing on the color green and why he likes it so much. What outfit will he wear when he gets up at six the next morning to make it to school in time to eat a free breakfast? Usually he just thinks whatever pops into his mind. For three years in a row, he says, he had the same dream. The one where his uncle Durell gets shot.

"I used to have these dreams when I was little," Diamond says, looking back on a life that's only ten years old. "That before he got shot he was here by this gas station. And I think he was walking. When he came out of the gas station he came out slowly and he looked ahead and then he looked around him. I think he saw somebody with a gun there. I think he was, like, running around. And when he had turned the corner the dream used to always cut off. I ain't never hear no more.

"The next day I'd have the same dream," Diamond continues. "Sometimes the dream would start from the point where it had ended the night before. It went that when he got around the corner he got shot. And he was on the floor. Then the man ran. And then I saw that somebody had called the police and they had asked him the name of my momma. I know they had to because my momma and sister came down to see him. That's it."

Diamond's uncle Durell lives in a dusty neighborhood close to the Broward County line. Durell's girlfriend answers the door and says she'll wake him. It's 10:30 in the morning on a Wednesday. The house's main room is dominated by a black leather couch. A stereo system in the corner features speakers with woofers larger than snare drums. On top of the stereo sit bottles of liquor: Bacardi, Cook's champagne, Heineken, and Red Dog beer. The walls are decorated with shards of glass; perhaps the glass missing from the main window, which is covered with a bedsheet. A wooden awning over the front door is collapsing. The door itself is so splintered it's possible to see through it to the street.

Getting Durell out of bed is a chore. He can make it from the bed to his wheelchair by himself, but without his girlfriend to lend a hand he can't overcome the six-inch step between the bedroom and the living room. With her assistance he rolls himself over the step. He asks her to bring him a glass of water.

Durell grew up in Miami. After graduating from Northwestern High, and with few other options he was aware of, he joined the Marines. He wishes he hadn't. "The Army's a lot easier," he says. "Once you get out of basic training the Army is pretty lax. Not so the Marine Corps."

Durell quit the Marines after two years. When he returned to Miami he took two jobs with the school system. During the day he filled out paperwork as a clerical assistant in the downtown office. At night he guarded a high school. He worked both jobs for two years. His combined income came nowhere near paying his bills.

"So this is me at twenty-two years old," he says as he relates his story. "I couldn't tell you what crack was or how to cut coke up or how to make some money on the corner. I was lame. But I was lured to the streets. It was the stuff that everybody had that I wanted and I knew I couldn't attain it with just a job. Or even two jobs."

A cousin agreed to mentor Durell in the drug trade. Like any apprentice, Durell began by simply hanging out, watching how his cousin operated. Making money seemed so easy that he started nickel-and-diming on the corner near his house. Nothing too big. Nothing, he learned, he was particularly cut out for. The game was all about trust, something Durell had a hard time fostering. Yet he kept trying. The lifestyle—money and the things it bought—were too seductive to give up.

"I was twenty-three when I got shot," he says. The events that landed Durell in his wheelchair are documented at the Miami-Dade County Criminal Courthouse in a manila folder nearly five inches thick. The initial incident took place on December 22, 1994.

It's kind of complicated. A girl had been robbed at gunpoint by a man named Melvin Saunders. The girl was tight with a friend of Durell's. The friend decided to avenge the robbery by killing Saunders. Durell, who lobbied for a less-final solution, accompanied his friend to the corner where they sold their drugs. Saunders was a neighborhood guy. He usually could be found on the streets late at night.

"Eventually we found him," Durell recalls. "And when we did, we cornered him, and he shot at us. I was trying to do a good thing, just trying to get my friend to settle his differences, but when we cornered Melvin he shot at us. He only shot at the ground, trying to back us off, but after he did that I was angry. I was like, 'I'm going to kill him.'"

Within a few hours, after the adrenaline wore off, Durell calmed down. He could have died, he realized, for nothing. He resolved to let things be. Unfortunately, Melvin Saunders didn't know that.

Two weeks passed. On January 3, 1995, Durell was walking in the neighborhood where he sold his drugs. He'd been hanging out with a friend and needed someone to drive him home. At a pay phone on a corner not far from the house where he's talking today, he called a girlfriend and asked for a ride. Saunders approached him from behind.

"As soon as I hung up the phone I knew something wasn't right," Durell states. "I heard somebody say: 'Y'all just couldn't let it be, huh? Y'all just couldn't leave well enough alone.' I could tell by the way he was talking that if I had maybe pleaded and said it wasn't me that I won't be shot. And I'm also thinking that if,

somehow, I get away from this situation, he out. Dead. I ain't
going to be taking no chances. He won't be sneaking up on me no
more."

Saunders sounded scared and nervous. Durell figured that he
shouldn't make any sudden moves. Finally, after five minutes standing at the phone listening to Saunders's threats, Durell decided to
slowly turn around. That's when Saunders fired his gun.

"I still don't believe his intentions were to shoot me, at least at
first," Durell says. "Even right when I was shot, when I was on the
ground, in my mind I was saying I didn't think he wanted to hit me.
I'd stopped, figuring he was just trying to scare me. That's when I
got hit in the lower back. Boom! I fell to the ground, paralyzed instantly. He ran up to me and put the gun on the back of my head. I
thought two things: one, that the barrel was kind of hot; two, that
this is it. I closed my eyes."

The gun jammed, sparing Durell's life. Sanders was eventually caught by the police. He was tried, convicted, and sentenced to
90-years-to-life in prison. Durell returned to the streets, this time
as a paraplegic.

"The sales came tenfold when I got in the chair," he says. "I
got more into drug dealing than ever. Business took off. A lot about
that is getting people to trust you. They see me and they figure, 'He
in a wheelchair, he ain't going to cross me up.'"

Durell no longer sells drugs, he insists; too many of his friends
have gone to jail, and he fears joining them. He takes a long sip of
his water and shifts in his chair. A UPS man pounds on the door of
a neighboring house. Durell considers his drug-dealing past to be
instructive, and that's why he's willing to talk about it. His past, and
the ease with which he fell into it, is a prime reason why he wants
Diamond to take football seriously.

"You get your kids into something to keep 'em out of the street,"
he says. "You know, it's not all a bad thing forcing these kids into
football. If you start 'em at an early age, eventually they learn, like,
you can't go to football without doing good in school. Football is a

good thing. If I had started off early in football I probably would have had a chance to go somewhere."

● ● ●

At the beginning of the season Durell lived with Diamond in Shakitha's apartment. He moved out about a month ago. Diamond misses him.

"He taught me how to iron my clothes when he was living here," Diamond says. "Of all the people I know I get along best with my uncle Durell. Like, when he plays with us he act just like a kid. He be playing all the games that we want to play. He had a Sega Dreamcast. We used to play that football game every morning before he used to go to work. Then at nighttime we just play the game for hours."

After four years in organized football, the past two with the Warriors, Diamond doesn't dream about Durell much anymore.

"Oh, last night I had a good dream!" Diamond remembers. "I was thinking about being a pro football player. They called me Diamond the Terminator or something like that. And I was making all these touchdowns and making all these interceptions and stuff and the crowd was going real wild and all that. Next thing you know the dream just went away. I don't know what happened. I fell asleep or something."

Chapter 5

Suniland

Phillip Thomas. Now there's a player. Brian Johnson and the other Warrior coaches knew about his performance on the 85s last year, playing tight end. They knew that the nine-year-old had the bulk and physical presence of a teenager, with a muscular torso and thick hair growing on his forearms. They knew full well that his brother, Clev'an, started at cornerback last season for Florida State. When Phillip's name didn't turn up on the preseason roster, Brian tracked him down at his aunt's house. After his aunt balked at paying the $75 it costs to register for the Warriors, Brian awarded Phillip a scholarship out of his own pocket.

"When Phillip say he going get that ball he's going to get that ball—and he's going to go through everybody to get that ball," says Phillip's aunt. "At least that's the way I seen him play. He got that type of . . . You know how them football players they have that toughness about them? They don't mess with them? That's where his attitude is at. He ain't going to get beat by these kids."

Adds Phillip's adult cousin, who lives with him: "He already got this mentality like he a high school star or whatever. He doesn't study in school. He says he can't go to tutoring because he has to go to football practice or whatever. He's getting it in his head that he's going to the pros."

At practice Friday Phillip showed where that attitude comes from. The Warriors offense had been sputtering and, as an experiment, the kids were told to switch positions and try different plays.

On his first play in the backfield Phillip took the small leather ball from Antwane, tucked it to his chest, and barreled clean through the defensive line. A boy named Red, one of the Warriors' more capable defenders, stood in front of Phillip like a traffic cop signaling for a stop. With a burst of speed, Phillip hammered straight ahead, toppling Red like a domino, unconscious.

"Phillip, he done lay Red out. He laid him out!" cheered assistant coach Chico as Brian and Coach Pete tried to revive the woozy defender. Sha-nise looked on approvingly. "Phillip's got a lot of hate in him," she said. "He mean. He got the hate in him."

Phillip lives near Hadley Park in a small house so old it's made of Dade County Pine, a construction material phased out in the twenties. After practice Phillip accepted a ride home from an assistant coach. He rode up 12th Avenue past the Amoco station on the corner where vendors sell T-shirts of Martin Luther King and Malcom X. Turning twice, the coach ended up at Phillip's aunt's house.

"My auntie, she raise me cause my momma wasn't raising me too good," Phillip says. His mother was, and still is, on drugs, real bad. Everyone who knows her describes her as wonderful. Everyone loves her. Everyone also acknowledges that she would disappear for days at a time from her home in the Liberty Square projects. Phillip was left to take care of himself until she came back, strung out and incapable of caring for even herself.

"He's a survivor," says Phillip's aunt, who has become his legal guardian. "He had to survive. He had to feed himself, get himself to school, dress himself. For instance, he always into food. Anytime he sees food he eats it. That's because to him if you don't eat you won't survive."

Phillip is the youngest (by more than a decade) of a host of talented siblings. One is a hairdresser, self-taught and so in demand for his skills that he never bothered to get a license. Phillip's oldest brother is an electrician. Another brother works on cars, or any kind of motor, actually—lawn mower, chain saw, whatever. Clev'an earned a degree in criminal justice at Florida State, becoming the first in the family to graduate from college. Phillip's father and mother were both infected with the AIDS virus at the time Phillip was conceived; his father has since died. Phillip has been tested frequently to see if he carries the virus himself. So far he's come up negative.

He is impatient to get on with his life.

"I got one, two, three, four, five, six, seven . . . no, eight more years of school," he says. "I can stand school but I can't wait to get out. I'm gonna get me a job, get me some money, money, money. Get me a J-O-B job."

What does he want to do?

"Play football! Since I was five that was my dream. I saw other people playing. They playing touch football and I asked 'em can I play football with 'em? So when I first played I loved it. My brother Clev'an, he played for FSU. He's supposed to be going to the NFL."

* * *

In his van, on the way to scout the Warriors' upcoming opponent, Brian and the other coaches can't stop talking about the videotape they watched last night, the one Brian's son shot at practice, the one that captures Phillip's emergence as a football force.

"Phillip laid Red out yesterday, a second-year player," marvels Chico, sitting on a plastic crate in the well between the front two bucket seats. "Red was playing safety, Phillip jiggled, Phillip dropped his helmet, stung him in his shoulder. That's the second second-year player he done laid out. Phillip's got lots of natural talent. Ain't never been tapped. We're going to get every inch out of him. Red is our best tackler in the secondary and Phillip just laid him out."

Brian joins the cheers. Beasley, too. Phillip's talent fuels everyone's optimism. The Georgia Southern offense may be taking longer to implement than had been hoped, but individual stars are emerging. Antwane's looking decent at quarterback. Andre seems to have the hands to make it as a receiver. DaQuan looks sharp on D. So does Red, even if Phillip did knock him unconscious.

The Goulds Rams will be the Warriors' first on-field adversary, next week. The Warriors usually assign at least one coach to scout the next team they'll play. Because of the Warriors' win by forfeit this week, the entire staff is free to scout the Rams on the road at Suniland, a park located in Pinecrest, the richest city in Miami-Dade County.

Pinecrest is a southern suburb, bordered by the Dixie Highway to the west and, to the east, by the waterfront palaces of Coral Gables. It's a bedroom community. Royal palms shade million-dollar mansions occupied by trial attorneys, bankers, plastic surgeons, and their children. Statistically, the median household income in Pinecrest is the highest in the state, and higher than 99 percent of all zip codes nationwide. The village is 30 percent Hispanic, 63 percent white, and just 2 percent black, with that black population half what it was ten years ago. One of five Suniland village councilmen is black, but then he's also a multimillion-dollar winner of the Florida Lottery.

Suniland Park sits on the western border of Pinecrest, abutting the strip malls of U.S. 1. The park is relatively small. There are two basketball courts, two red-dirt softball diamonds, and one football field crammed between the highway and a home plate. The Warriors commandeer a picnic bench in one of the few patches of shade available. Midway through the first half, all-black Goulds has failed to score on Suniland, a team of smaller, primarily white boys.

"We gonna kill 'em first game. They got no speed!" cheers Chico, leaping off the picnic bench after a Goulds running back is stuffed for a loss. Beasley, in a gray softball T-shirt, stores his growing optimism on a microcassette. "We'll be in a no-huddle by the fifth game," he whispers into a tiny tape recorder.

* * *

Type "Suniland Sundevils" into a search engine and up will come a Web-based shrine sponsored by a Miami law firm. Posted on the Web site are pictures of both national championship Suniland teams, including the infamous midgets from last season. Those 145-pounders are pictured at the park, their orange jerseys as bright as the sun splashing their eyes. The site features close-up shots of the national championship trophy, the Greater Miami Pop Warner championship trophy, and of the gold-and-orange-and-black national championship rings awarded to every player on the team. A separate page details the accomplishments of starting quarterback Tommy Hoffman. Yet another page lists the name, number, and position of each player on the team, along with a photo of each player's face.

To anyone familiar with the village of Suniland, the parade of players, one face after another, is curious. All of the players are black. Almost all of them, anyway—just six of the twenty-eight Sundevils who played on the national championship team in 2000 were white. That's a complete inversion of the racial demographics of Suniland itself. A historically losing team in a wealthy and overwhelmingly white park has won two national championships in a row on the speedy legs of black players imported from other neighborhoods.

Pop Warner football has been played in Miami for more than thirty years. The league remained functionally segregated until the late eighties. Before integration, Suniland was a winning program. The Sundevils, whatever the weight class, captured a healthy share of city championships. Then, eleven years ago, Liberty City entered the league and everything changed.

"We used to call it Little Bighorn," says one Suniland coach of his team's visits to Liberty City, "because every time we went there we were slaughtered."

Suniland teams are still slaughtered—most of them, anyway. Most of the weight classes in the park remain stocked with white suburban boys. Nearly every week they lose. The league frowns on blowouts, and has instituted rules to prevent lopsided final scores, yet it's common for a Sundevils team to lose by margins of twenty points.

"If I was a coach that ended up in Liberty City or Goulds, I would feel I had died and gone to heaven," says the Suniland coach. "My God, to have what they have, the talent."

Then a white coach named Gator Rebhan showed up at Suniland, and what the inner city always had—speed—ended up in the suburbs. With an infusion of athleticism, Rebhan's Suniland teams were instantaneously transformed into national powers. In its very first year with Rebhan as head coach, Suniland—if only his one team at Suniland—marched through its schedule without a loss. The Sundevils became the Sioux; former bullies such as Liberty City turned into Custer's cavalry.

In Orlando, in 1999, Rebhan's team won a national title at the 125-pound junior midget weight division. The same group of boys went back to Disney in 2000 and secured the 145-pound championship with a defeat of the Marshall Heights Bison, from Washington, D.C. Park officials, giddy with unfamiliar success, commissioned a sign, erected to face busy Dixie Highway: "Home of the two-time undefeated national champion Suniland Sundevils."

Marshall Heights had arrived in Orlando also undefeated and unscored upon. When the pregame fireworks exploded and the honorary captains from the NFL flipped the coin and the national anthem rang out and the red lights flared on the television cameras broadcasting the game nationally, the men from Pop Warner's national office awaited a great contest, their marquee marketing event.

Unfortunately, the Bison were absolutely no match for the Sundevils. The team representing the poshest suburb of Miami gained yards at will. Quarterback Tommy Hoffman threw three touchdowns in the first half. By halftime the score stood 40–6. Those same Pop Warner officials who'd been expecting a great advertisement for their league stepped in for damage control. Before the teams took the field for the second-half kickoff, Rebhan was warned not to run up the score. Specifically, he was ordered not to throw any more passes.

Rebhan's team passed the ball anyway. Some witnesses say members of the Marshall team, in their humiliation, had started playing dirty, trying to injure Sundevils players. Rebhan had no choice but to look out for his players' collective safety, it is argued. He had no choice but to order a 24-yard pass in the fourth quarter that a speedy receiver carried untouched to the pristine turf of the Disney World Sports Complex end zone.

Even with a running clock, the game could not end quickly enough. When the final gun fired on a lopsided 56–6 Suniland win, Rebhan and his team huddled at midfield, celebrating their status as the best Pop Warner team in the country. Each player received a gold medallion hung on a red-white-and-blue ribbon. Rebhan hoisted aloft a trophy. Then he returned to Miami, where, in his mailbox, he found a letter from Ron Dilatesh, national football commissioner for Pop Warner Little Scholars, Inc.

"It is the determination of the National Office," wrote Dilatesh, "that at the recently concluded Pop Warner Super Bowl, as head Coach of the Suniland Sundevils, you intentionally ran up the score in the Midget Championship game.

"Based on my personal observations and discussions with others present, you violated the rules . . . by passing late in the game with your team well ahead. This occurred after being spoken to . . . twice about trying to keep scoring to a minimum.

"Therefore, you are suspended indefinitely as a volunteer in the Pop Warner program. Any future involvement would be subject to approval by the National Office, as well as Regional and League officials."

Mark Peterson, the president of the Greater Miami chapter of Pop Warner, applauded the decision. "Our only regret," he says, "is that national got to him first. We were about to do something ourselves."

🏈 🏈 🏈

After he was stripped of his Suniland coaching privileges, Rebhan complained that the rest of Miami, along with the rest of America, was jealous of his success. They banned him from coaching, he said, only because his teams couldn't be stopped on the field. That opinion, dismissed by Pop Warner officials, remains the conventional wisdom at Suniland Park.

"The main thing is Gator took a white park and did good," says a Suniland coach. "You're not supposed to do that. Black parks rule. White parks are supposed to lay down and such. That's what really pissed them off. All of Miami—hell, the whole country—hates Suniland."

Eric Stephens is the Suniland football commissioner. He has short legs, a trim brown beard, and a day job running the Miami MetroZoo. The lobby of the building where he works is protected by a stuffed white Bengal tiger. Inside his office, among photos of other zoo animals, are snapshots of a boy in a football uniform. Like most adults who oversee Pop Warner, Stephens got involved on the heels of his son, a quarterback.

"I tell him that winning is important," Stephens says. "I tell him that winning requires commitment and hard work. I push him harder than I push anyone else."

Stephens responded to the ruling against his star coach with a letter to Commissioner Dilatesh. After opining that Rebhan's suspension "appears to have been made in haste and without benefit of review," Stephens raised niggling questions about the play during the championship game. Why did Suniland even have the ball in the second half if Pop Warner rules state that, in a rout, the losing team retains possession until it narrows the score gap? How could Rebhan have been running up the score if there was only one offensive touchdown in the second half? Stephens asked for a list of coaches "against whom the national office has taken this action in the past."

Dilatesh did not respond in a way Stephens found encouraging.

"My first reaction is disappointment because nowhere in your letter do you accept any responsibility for the actions of Mr. Rebhan," Dilatesh wrote back. The commissioner reiterated that he had talked to Rebhan during and after the game, and that the coach understood he was barred from throwing any more passes. The suspension remained in effect.

So Rebhan sued to get his volunteer job back. Predictably, a host of sportswriters pounced on the story. Even *Sports Illustrated* ran a blurb. Usually the reports were couched in mock-apocalyptic terms, like, What is this world coming to when people take Pop Warner football so seriously?

"Lawsuits . . . national championships . . . coast-to-coast TV broadcasts. Know what's really wrong with this picture?" asked a writer at the *Seattle Times.* "We're talking about thirteen- and fourteen-year-old boys here."

The matter remains in legal dispute. With Rebhan banned from coaching, most players fled Suniland Park to play for programs more likely to visit Disney World. Only a dozen kids showed up for the first day of practice, less than half a normal team. Rather than teach those twelve boys how to persevere in the face of adversity, park commissioner Eric Stephens chose to scrap the team altogether. There is no 145-pound team playing for Suniland this season.

"We felt it would be a disservice to the kids to field a team that wasn't competitive every game," says a Suniland official.

Stephens knows his park is developing a reputation as a sort of Evil Empire, that it is seen as having sold its soul to win. When Mark Peterson tried to curb recruiting by forcing kids to play at the parks nearest their home addresses, Suniland was the only park to vote against the measure.

"We fought the boundary issue because it was a matter of public fairness," Stephens elaborates. "The law says I can go where I like and play football. We didn't think it was an appropriate rule."

Because Suniland successfully blocked the rule, Sundevil coaches remain free to recruit. Stephens is not in any way opposed to this development. Busing blacks into the park allows his son to play on a racially mixed team, which is a good learning experience, he says. Besides, these imported recruits mean the Sundevils have to endure fewer blowout losses.

"Winning breeds confidence in kids," Stephens explains. "Players on a team that goes 0–9 will feel differently about themselves than a team that goes 5–5. Those that never win don't feel good about themselves. It's a bad experience."

Chapter 6

Goulds

Not long after the founding of Miami, when disease and over-crowding defined Nigger Town, a few pioneering blacks struck out on their own. With money saved from low-paying construction jobs, thirty-five families carved out a homestead in one of the few places they could buy land, an isolated block near the Florida East Coast rail yard. The settlers built simple homes with tar paper roofs. Black-owned businesses emerged to serve the new neighborhood's needs.

Over the next forty years, as Miami grew more prosperous and populous, whites began encroaching on the Railroad Shop, as the black settlement came to be known. By the late 1940s, the black enclave stood as an island surrounded on all sides by the middle-class white neighborhood of Allapattah. In 1947, the school board, looking for a place to build a new, all-white middle school, voted to eliminate the island altogether. A county judge granted a condemnation request. Sixty families were living in the Railroad Shop at the time.

On a morning of steady rain, as most residents labored at their jobs, county workers evicted nearly the entire neighborhood. Every possession in almost every home was dumped outside on the wet ground. Doors and windows were boarded up. Signs posted on the doors warned against trespassing. The evicted included Brian Johnson's father, who built a new house in the dense brush four miles north. Two of the elder Johnson's brothers moved far south. Another brother moved north to the Broward County line.

Two years after the mass eviction, the county commandeered the rest of the Railroad Shop for a public park. No one had to be evicted, as the few blacks who remained knew what was in store for them. Manor Park became home to a quasi-pro softball league. All the players were white.

By 1980, the neighborhood had turned back. Blockbusting in Allapattah and subsequent white flight made homes around the park attractive again to blacks. Brian's dad returned to a house one block from Manor Park, which was soon renamed Hadley Park after the leader of a black get-out-the-vote drive.

"He just wanted to move back to his old neighborhood," Brian says. "He never wanted to leave in the first place, and he came back here as soon as he could."

Brian spent his youth in Hadley Park scaling mounds of dirt that were later flattened into the current football practice fields. He played basketball on the courts and spun lap after lap on the park's outdoor concrete roller rink. Thin metal guardrails circled the rink to restrain anyone skating so fast they threatened to spin right off the banked oval.

Ed, the Warriors' offensive line coach, sits atop one of those rails. He reads Bible passages out of a paper pamphlet so small he may have found it inside a box of Cracker Jack. His yellow Warriors game polo rests on a knee. With breath that stinks of cigarettes he repeats a mantra five times before closing the pamphlet: "God be merciful on this sinner." He hops off the rail, pulls on his polo, and wades into the crowd of boys gathering on the uneven roller-rink concrete.

"We going down *south*," says Stevie, a cornerback who idolizes Deion Sanders so much he mimics the former NFL superstar in attitude and in ghetto-fabulous jewelry (in Stevie's case forged of plastic). "We got a long way to go to play today, but that's okay; I got people down there. Let me say this right now: We go down there and get our butts kicked we ain't never comin' back." Stevie wears jersey number 22, in honor of his idol. When it's pointed out that Sanders wore number 21, Stevie looks down at his uniform for five seconds, then looks up sheepishly.

"I guess I made a mistake," he says softly, his attitude temporarily muted.

All the Warriors are accounted for. Diamond Pless drops his black-and-yellow equipment bag on the concrete and scales a guardrail. Other players remove hip and thigh pads from their practice pants and stuff them into the pockets of their clean black game pants. Socks and pads are tossed into duffel bags. Coach Beasley uses a straightened wire coat hanger to push belts through pant loops.

Antwane, the quarterback, doesn't need a belt looped through his game pants. In the preliminary team weigh-in Antwane tipped the scale about a pound too heavy. Actually, he was right on the line at 95½-pounds, but the coaches won't take chances with their most important player. If a boy weighs more than he's supposed to, even a half-pound more, he can't play in the game. Antwane is ordered to walk around the basketball courts under the supervision of Coach Ed.

Antwane shuffles laps wearing plastic sandals, a white T-shirt, and cargo shorts. His flak jacket—armor that some quarterbacks wear to protect their ribs—dangles unclipped from his shoulders. A "V" of sweat rises between his shoulder blades. Terrance, a player carrying what has been diagnosed as a half-pound of water weight, laps Antwane twice before Coach Ed notices and tells Terrance to slow down lest he spend strength he needs in the game.

"They talkin' about he right on the borderline," Ed spits, referring to Antwane. "How can he be on the borderline? He should know better. These boys are kids. They ain't got no discipline yet." Ed has his own sons, one of whom plays for the 110s. He doesn't have any problems maintaining *their* weight. "My one son, he was four pounds heavy so I fed him Crystal Light, a head of lettuce, and two cans of tuna fish every day. By the first game he was right on. Lost four pounds just like that."

*   *   *

The drive down U.S. 1 is a long parade of car dealerships, all flying rows of nylon American flags. Every two miles or so the fast-food restaurants recycle—Wendy's, KFC, McDonald's and back again. Eventually the strip malls thin out. Fields of tomatoes and strawberries open up. In a crowded, urban county, southern Miami-Dade retains a connection to the land.

Two black settlers founded Goulds nearly a century ago. While the rich soil made the land ideal for growing produce, the entrepreneurs cultivated landowners instead, selling much of their property to other blacks. The unincorporated city remains predominantly black to this day. It also remains poor: The median household income in Goulds is about half the county average.

To house the poorest of these people, the county erected compounds of publicly subsidized town houses. Goulds Park sits directly across the street from the largest project. The park features a running track of crushed rubber, soccer fields for the growing Hispanic population, basketball courts, a football field with lights, and, as the centerpiece, a new field house like the one in Gwen Cherry Park, built like that one with NFL money donated in conjunction with a Super Bowl. The Goulds Park football program took its nickname—the Rams—and its colors—red and gray—from Mays High, a black school closed since desegregation.

"Goulds is a tough place to play," says Brian Johnson as the bus pulls into the park. "In '98, our national year, there had to be a million fans there—dope smokers, dealers. They harassed us the whole game. It got pretty scary. We won, but when the game was over we realized we were outnumbered and just got out of there quick as we could."

Floodlights already shine on the field, which is painted fresh for the first home game of the season. Gangs of rail-thin men amble out of the town houses. They wear wife-beater tank tops and shorts so baggy and so long they can be tripped over. The men cheer on the Goulds 85-pounders, who have just scored a late touchdown to take the lead over the Warriors in the evening's undercard.

The pregame weigh-in for the 95s is conducted in a bathroom at the park's field house. The Warriors stand in one line, the older-but-lighters first. These are the handful of eleven-year-olds so slight of build they're allowed another season with the 95s. For this game the older-but-lighters must weigh no more than 76 pounds. (The weight limit for all players increases one pound per week during the season.) The scale is set at 76 pounds. If the level clanks the top of the scale, the player is disqualified. Clarence, who was so close to the edge he'd been walking laps with Antwane, makes the cut. So, eventually, does Antwane, along with everyone else.

The Warriors gather in a circle to stretch. Stevie lies on his back as Coach Beasley pushes on one of his legs to loosen the hamstring. Beasley has written down his prediction of exactly how the game will unfold. On paper it looks spectacular. The Warriors will score a touchdown on their first play. The offense will score 35 points in all. If the Warriors defense does its job and scores a TD of its own, the final score should be—make that *will be*—48–0.

"Everybody always expects a team in Pop Warner to open cautiously," Beasley says as he grasps Stevie's ankle. "Our wide receiver, he has a green light to go for the goal. That's going to light the fuse. Antwane will go straight back and throw it. They won't be expecting that."

Stevie switches legs.

"I see it," Beasley says, grabbing Stevie's airborne cleat with both hands. "I see the touchdown already."

Head coach Brian Johnson slips on his game shirt. The Warrior coaches wear yellow polos, black shorts, and shiny black dress sneakers. Because it's the first game of the season, Brian's clothes are clean. That won't necessarily be the case as the year progresses.

"I feel every team need a little luck," he explains. "It don't matter how good your talent is or how good you coach, you still need to catch a break. So I try to make my own break. Our championship year a bird shit right here." Brian points to his left breast. "I kept that all year. I'd show up every game with two shirts. Right before kickoff I take off my clean shirt and put on the one I'd been wearing, even though it had the bird shit on it. I'm a little superstitious in order to get chance to fall my way."

On the field, the 85-pound Warriors, trailing by a point, are down to their last play. A wobbly Hail Mary pass tossed up the middle is caught somehow by a Warrior receiver, who chugs ninety yards downfield for the winning touchdown.

"Shit!"

"Fuck!" Expletives fall from the home bleachers. The Warriors' 95s, waiting in the end zone, are roused by the last-second victory. Players clank their yellow helmets, slap shoulder pads, and bounce like pogo sticks. Assistant coach Chico exhorts the team to turn it loose: "This is for real, men. We ain't gonna take the foot off the gas. Pop Warner gonna have to come see me on Tuesday," he says, indicating that the Warriors are going to run up the score so high he's going to be in trouble with the league.

"This is real time, men," says Coach Ed, who's donned a black leather baseball cap he wears only during games. "This is where you show what you have on the field, right here."

Stevie leads the call and response:

Liberty City got a dog pound!
 Woof! Woof!

Goulds Rams got a cat sound!
 Meow! Meow!

What time is it?
 Showtime!

What time is it?
 Showtime!

The 95s sprint from the end zone through a gauntlet of cheerleaders and 85-pound park mates. "Time to play some ball!" shouts a father standing behind the yellow rope that separates the spectators from the coaches and players. Brian stakes out a position on the sideline, crouched as if he were a baseball catcher, his hands resting on his thighs. Coach Beasley huddles with the offense. He's down on one knee, scripting the opening drive on a white dry-erase board. While he runs through his plan of attack, Goulds runs through the Warriors defense for a touchdown. Liberty City is losing 6–0 when the Warriors' offense touches the ball for the first time.

This is the moment Beasley has been waiting a year for. This is the play he's announced in advance. The Goulds defenders will be thinking run. There's no way they're expecting a quarterback only ten years old to throw an accurate bomb thirty yards down the field. Even if they thought Antwane could throw the ball that far there's no way Sedrick, the receiver, will be open. Or so Beasley wants them to think.

"We're going to score a touchdown on the first play," he says again, for at least the tenth time today.

This is what actually happens: Sedrick manages to get open, just as Beasley predicted. But Antwane throws the ball well over the receiver's head and so far out of bounds it grazes the leaves of a black olive tree hanging above the bleachers. Incomplete. Beasley stares at the field as if he has just returned home, flipped on the lights, and discovered that all his furniture has been stolen. On subsequent plays, Antwane ignores the color-coded diagrams on his wrist and runs the wrong way, always straight into Goulds linebackers. Phillip fumbles to start the second quarter. By halftime the Warriors have yet to score.

"Y'all not listenin'," rails Beasley as the offense kneels in the end zone, sucking orange slices and scratching their heads. "Y'all trying to make up your minds on your own. This game is so easy to win, if you want to win. They're leaving wide-open holes for us.

"Antwane, twice you went the wrong way. Antwane! What's going on, man? DaQuan, where you at? You with us? Brandon, you got to get your head up—it's wide open! Sedrick, you turned all around. Everyone out of place. Diamond is the only one standing in the right place, ready to play. I got to go searching for the rest of y'all. It's mental stuff."

Diamond may be in the right place on the plays, but he hasn't exactly been part of the action. Beasley is so worried about Diamond dropping the ball he hasn't asked Antwane to even look in the receiver's direction. Not that Antwane could hit Diamond if he tried. Brian takes the quarterback aside. The head coach places his hands on Antwane's shoulder pads and stares him in the eye.

"They can't stop you," Brian says. "Who stopped you? Tell me that. You. You stopped you. You noticed that, right?"

Antwane nods his head. He doesn't say anything. In the second half he continues to turn in the wrong directions. Goulds runs up the score.

* * *

The referee administers two long breaths to his whistle, ending Liberty City's first game of the season. Warriors pull off their helmets to reveal tear-soaked cheeks. Reluctantly, they line up to shake the hands of the victorious Rams, then gather at midfield.

"Take a knee, men," says Brian. Brandon is crying. So is Chase, a receiver. "It takes hard work, men! Hard work. Some of y'all want to do it. Some of you don't. You played a little too much before the game. Got to stay focused."

Brian glares down at his players. Their streaming tears temper his anger. "All right," he says quietly. "One loss will not kill us, gentlemen. One loss will not kill us."

The Warriors strip off their jerseys and pants right on the field. Antwane's grandfather apologizes to Beasley for Antwane's performance, saying his grandson seemed burnt-out from dropping weight before the game. Beasley counters that Antwane needs to focus on the offensive game plan, which, he asserts, even after tonight's debacle, remains foolproof. Beasley follows Antwane to the bus, first grabbing a biscuit, a piece of fried chicken, and an orange drink a team mother packed in a cooler.

Brian remains at midfield. He stuffs dirty jerseys into a black mesh bag.

"That's the way the cookie crumbles," he says.

That simple?

"Yeah, it's that simple."

Chapter 7

September 11

"After we lose, I can't watch football," says the Warriors' Brian Johnson as he slumps into the soft folds of his living room couch. *Apocalypse Now* plays on the television. "I can't watch any football. The only football I'd watch is the Hurricanes or something like that—I *got* to watch them. But otherwise, I don't watch football at all."

Brian's son eats generic Froot Loops at a small round table in the kitchen. The way the house is laid out, with the kitchen virtually in the living room and the bedrooms all crammed together close, it's possible to hear every crunched Loop, even with the sound on the movie cranked high. Sha-nise roams from her bedroom, past the TV, outside for a minute, then back inside to her bedroom. A friend of Brian's wife drops in, heels clicking on the white tile floor.

Brian's house sits within eyesight of the bungalow canyons of the Liberty Square housing complex. It's a straight drive up Northwest 12th Avenue from Hadley Park, past a Taco Bell where the workers assemble *chalupas* behind bullet-proof glass. His house lies outside the concrete wall that once marked the boundaries of the black community, though the wall still stands and Brian lives close enough that he could almost hit it with an avocado plucked from his backyard tree. Brian inherited the house after one of his aunts died.

"This is a ghetto home," he says flatly. "But I don't worry about security none. I don't have bars on the window. My brother says in this neighborhood all you got to do is every once in a while go out into your backyard and fire your gun into the air. Then you walk to the front yard, let everyone see your gun, and then you go back into your house and you don't worry about nothing."

Brian was born in Miami Beach. His parents are of what he calls "Georghamian" descent. His mother's family moved down from Georgia to work the construction jobs available during the post-WWII building boom. His father's father was one of thousands of islanders who fled economic collapse in the Bahamas. Brian considers himself a Miamian, purebred.

Twenty years ago, when he enrolled at Northwestern High School—a state football power famous for delivering a steady stream of 250-pound linebackers to Florida's best college programs—Brian stood so skinny he didn't bother trying out for the team. Size wasn't the only factor—there was also all that structure. Not just in sports, but in school itself. He didn't like the way teachers told him what to do, or the way his classmates seemed uninterested in anything they were supposedly being taught. For all its athletic prowess, Northwestern has long held one of the worst academic reputations in the state. Brian saw no reason to mark his time.

"I wanted to be out of there," he recalls. "My first and second year I took nothing but the requirements. In my first semester they had me taking something like piano. I was like, 'No, no, back that up, get that out of there.' I had friends who had two PE classes. What? What you be taking two PE for? I just wanted out. By the eleventh grade I was working full-time. I'd go to school until noon, then I'd work."

Work entailed cleaning the kennels of the Flagler dog track, a decaying greyhound circuit set in the endless pavement of Little Havana, a venue more popular for its Saturday flea market than for any action on its dirt oval. He also worked the kennels at a second dog track near the Broward County border. "I did everything with those fucking dogs," he recalls. "I cleaned them up, fed them, took care of them, muzzled them, shoveled up their shit."

Brian's family believes in education. His mother earned a master's degree when she was in her sixties. Brian briefly explored earning a college degree of his own, largely to appease his father.

He signed up for classes at Miami-Dade Community College, located across from the football stadium where Northwestern plays most of its games. He thought he might be interested in becoming a veterinarian.

"It wasn't for me," he says of his college career, which lasted only two semesters. "I saw the same bunch of people I had spent all that time trying to get away from. The trouble was I had just bought all my books. They cost something like five hundred dollars, and my dad had put up the money. I had something like six hundred dollars in the bank, and that was all I had in my name. I went up to my dad, gave him five hundred dollars and said, 'Hey, Dad, sorry, but this college thing just ain't for me.' I was down to my dick, you know what I'm saying? I didn't have nothing else left but what I could hold in my hand. Borrowing that money and going to college was the biggest mistake I ever made."

It took little time for Brian to recover from his mistake. He rose to assistant paddock judge at the Flagler track, a job that kept him out of the hot sun. While going to a movie with friends, he was set up with Althea Gibson. They had a son. Then they got married, when Brian was twenty-one. He quit the track and took his current job with a small company that delivers nuts, bolts, and washers to warehouses operated by Publix supermarkets and others. His wife works as a nurse at Jackson Hospital, where their daughter was born.

"I started with the Warriors in '93," Brian says. "My son wanted to play. He was seven. After school he was coming home and chilling out, the same old thing every day. I was riding by Hadley Park and I see them practicing and I say, 'Oh man, I think we ought to try this out.' They had so many kids they had to make three teams, A, B, and C. The guy coaching the C team needed an assistant coach so I said, 'All right, I'm going to help out.'"

$$\text{\textit{⚈ ⚈ ⚈}}$$

The Warriors lost their second game in a row, at home, to Florida City. Rain soaked the field. Fat drops of water rolled off Brian's black

Warriors visor until he whipped it off his head in disgust. He had reason to be frustrated. Throughout the first half his defense incurred penalty after penalty. On offense, Antwane overthrew his receivers again. Phillip showed absolutely nothing at running back, same as in the Goulds game. Phillip's replacement in the backfield failed his audition, initially lining up in the wrong spot, then fumbling on his first carry.

"They not playing with no heart," assistant coach Chico said at halftime. "We need to see the Wizard of Oz, 'cept I don't have his phone number."

At halftime, while the Warrior coaches searched for signs of life, a player named Dion distracted himself from the game by consuming three hot dogs and a can of strawberry soda. This did not help him play better. Midway through the third quarter, just about the time the visiting Razorbacks scored another touchdown, Dion's epic snack caught up with him, violently. He fell to the ground in a convulsion, his ten-year-old body twitching in pain. The coaches stared at Dion's shock reaction, frozen with shock of their own.

"He needs a paper bag or something," Beasley finally said. Dion grabbed on to Brian's ankle. Rainwater fell between lips quivering in agony. Paramedics from a firehouse located behind the field came out to cart Dion away.

Brian went with him, first to the fire station and then to Jackson Hospital (where the problem was diagnosed as severe indigestion). As he walked off the field with Dion and the paramedics, the rain that soaked him mixed with a stream of criticism.

"It's the coaches' fault!" he was heckled by a man standing alongside the fence that rings the field. "It's the coaches' fault when they don't do on Saturday what they learn during the week. . . . And what is he doing leaving the field when they all still playin'? . . . Brian ain't no head coach. He a quitter, that what he is."

Inside the fire station, Brian shook himself dry. From where he was standing he could see his defeated players trudging off the muddy field. The next weight class stomped through mud puddles as they prepared for their game to start. Brian stood 1–2 as a head coach, with that one win coming via forfeit.

"I dunno," he said. "I tried to be nice to them. I tried to yell at them. I'm 'bout ready to split their head open with an axe, put it back together, and see if that gets through to them."

Catastrophe. Disaster. The words bandied about after the Florida City loss were notable in their severity. It was as if two losses in a season, at this level of football, were the end of the world. Brian don't know how to coach. Brian a damn fool. Beasley offense too complicated. Devastating! Terrible! Horrible! The harsh judgments softened little the following Tuesday, when four airplanes took off from airports in Boston and Washington. Hijackers used the planes to kill more than three thousand people in the most spectacular mass murder in American history. Miami, like the rest of the country, stopped still. Offices shut down. Gyms closed. Mothers rushed home to hug their children. Families gathered in front of the TV to watch the endless, unspeakable replays of the World Trade Center disintegrating in a shower of concrete, steel, and human flesh.

At Palmetto Field, the Raiders held practice as usual.

"I figured that's what we're supposed to do, go on with our lives," said Coach Campos afterward. "With all due respect to the dead, I felt it was our job to keep going and not let them disrupt our lives. It was a pretty lousy practice, like usual on a Tuesday."

At Hadley Park, assistant cheerleading coordinator Tangela Stanley stands in the parking lot closest to the practice fields, shooing cars away. "No practice today," she says to the driver of a green Honda, two tiny football players in full equipment gazing out the rear window. The park is closed. A few of the 110s wait in vain on a picnic bench, as if the decision to cancel might be reversed at any minute. Charlie, a young assistant in the Warriors front office, leans against a black Lexus with gold rims. A clutch of middle-aged men keeps him company. One man munches boiled peanuts. Another man, in a black Liberty City baseball cap, sips from a sixteen-ounce can of Budweiser sheathed in a brown paper bag.

"I didn't know the Pentagon was a building in Washington," Charlie says. "I thought it was a military something. Turns out it's just an office building."

"I'm forty years old and I ain't never been on a plane," says the beer drinker in the baseball hat.

"I'm not saying it's all right to knock down those buildings," offers the peanut eater. "But I can see why they did it. Those people out there have no visibility. They have no way to protest."

The words hang out there. The peanut eater chomps a few nuts. The beer drinker draws a sip. In this park, in Liberty City, there isn't much identification with the dead.

"We play Overtown next week," Charlie says. "They be calling us up today, they was calling the office. They say they gonna do the same thing to us. They say, 'We gonna drop a bomb on you.'"

"That's sick," Charlie says with a smile too wide to hide his approval.

A car rolls into the lot. When it stops a young man pops open the driver's-side door. He is wearing a FUBU polo shirt, jeans baggy enough to camp in, and the kind of Nikes that go "boing!" Dreadlocks fall to his elbows. All his teeth gleam gold. A bulky platinum watch blings on his wrist. His face is long and skinny, much like his muscular torso.

"Park's closed," Tangela informs him.

"What the fuck?" he says, opening his door wider. The film *Rush Hour* plays on a dashboard TV. "This here's a ghetto park."

Maurice Robinson slowly rolls the car into one of the many available parking spaces. He is twenty-five years old, unemployed, and the father of five boys with four different women. His criminal record features two dozen arrests for a variety of nonviolent crimes. On the soft end: misdemeanor loitering, cannabis possession, and possession of stolen property. More seriously: felony cocaine possession with intent to distribute and felony burglary. The first time he was shot, in the abdomen, he was fourteen.

Robinson lets his oldest son, age seven, leap out and run around. He turns off the movie and tries to tune in a local news station.

Dashboard TVs being what they are, he can pick up only a fuzzy replay of the collapse of the North Tower. He looks at the screen for a while, then turns toward the empty playing fields. Thumb-sized dragonflies strafe clusters of crabgrass. A paper cup tumbles toward the baseball diamond. Robinson shoots a short, coarse laugh that rattles his dreadlocks.

"It ain't like they gonna bomb this all here," he says.

Chapter 8

McAdoo

On Thursday nights after practice Brian Johnson visits the mobile home that serves as the Warriors' temporary clubhouse. Tonight, after stepping inside, he pulls the whistle from his neck and sets it down on the surface of a folding table.

"Where are the jerseys?" he asks an assistant. After being pointed to a closet, Brian scavenges until he finds the appropriate black mesh bag. At some parks, every player gets to keep his jersey after the season ends. The Warriors operate a tighter ship. Rather than buy new helmets, for instance, the Warriors recondition their headgear for a fraction of the cost. And rather than spend money on new jerseys every year, the Warriors keep the uniforms in-house, launder them themselves, and reuse them season after season.

Brian unties the knot atop the bag, dumps onto the floor a pile of black jerseys with yellow numbers, and pulls up a metal folding chair. He's checking to see that every player on his team will have a uniform when they show up at the game on Saturday, and that the jersey number will match the number assigned on the roster. When he pulls out number 11 he checks off Antwan's name. Number 33 for Diamond. Number 8 for Phillip, the same number Phillip's brother wore at Florida State. When Brian has laid out all the jerseys and checked them against his list, one jersey is missing. This won't cause him a problem come game time. That jersey, number 61, is always missing. Since linebacker Martin Wright wore it for the national championship team in 1998, no one has worn it again. Number 61 has been retired.

"Number Siiiiiiiiixty-oooooone!" Brian bellows, drawing out each digit for a full and reverential two seconds. He purses his lips and blows out air in a slow, low whistle. "That's Martin," he says finally. "Martin . . . Martin . . . What's his name? Martin Wright! Mar! Tin! Wright! That boy was *awesome.* He was *The One...*" Brian doesn't complete his sentence. Instead he conjures up a memory of the boy's unbelievable fifteen tackles and six sacks in the national championship game, and his team-leading thirty-one sacks in one season—three times more sacks than the rest of the Warriors combined.

"He's supposed to be playing with the 145s this year," Brian says when he snaps back to consciousness. "He ain't out here 'cause his grades ain't what they supposed to be. I went out and talked to his mother. I sat down with her for two hours. She tell me he want to play the clown in class. I looked at his report card from this year; I looked at his report cards from last year. And I agree: He shouldn't be playing."

Brian stuffs the jerseys back in the bag, every number save 61 present and accounted for. The Warriors will wear black jerseys and black pants on Saturday in what will be a 12–7 loss to the Overtown Rattlers, the Warrior's third defeat in a row. But preparing for that dismal future is not what Brian is thinking about now.

"But I'm telling you, man," Brian adds, pulling tight the bag's drawstring, "he was the one. The One. That boy could play.

"Martin's father is McAdoo. You know the deal with him, right?"

McAdoo leans over the counter separating his kitchen from his living room. His left hand pins a sheet of white poster board to a weathered orange countertop. His right hand drags a red Magic Marker across the surface of the poster, drawing the letters of a giant greeting card for the commissioner of the Warriors program. "To Sam: Get well soon."

The poster is coming along slowly. McAdoo started it last night, and would have had it finished had the green leather couch facing the TV not demanded a snooze. Now, at nearly noon, his motor skills aren't yet sharp. His face puffs around the eyes and jowls. He's wearing what he fell asleep in, what he wears every day: a gray polyester Dickies work shirt and a matching pair of Dickies polyester pants. Clipped to the lapel of the shirt is a yellow button he made when his son returned from Disney World three years ago: "National Champs."

"Bragging rights," he says, not looking up from his poster. "That's what football all about. We're talking about *serious* bragging rights. Come February on, that's all we do. We be hanging out with Luke Campbell or Edgerrin James or Randy Moss or Dante Culpepper and our big NFL players down here and all we'll be talking about is what our sons did last season."

He looks up from the poster and jabs a finger as if pointing it in the face of an opposing father.

"Your son *sucks!*" he taunts. "Know what I mean?"

McAdoo lives in an almond-painted house on a shadeless street a mile east of Hadley Park. Next door a compound of public housing units stands behind a chainlink fence. The inside of his house is so dark it's hard to judge the poster's artistic merits. The primary illumination comes from a television broadcasting a *SportsCenter* marathon. A skyline of his son's trophies rises from a glass coffee table. Store-bought posters line every wall. Martin Luther King, Nelson Mandela, Malcolm X. The most prominent poster hangs in a hallway near the bathroom. Edgerrin James, the running back for the Indianapolis Colts and a former standout at the University of Miami, has signed the poster, which features his uniformed likeness. "To Mike, keep it REAL, EJ."

McAdoo doesn't own a high profile. His real name, Michael Wright, has appeared in the *Miami Herald* exactly once, and only then for a quote about how proud he was of his son's national title. Yet from Liberty City to West Perrine he is well-known, almost a public figure. He has juice. Politicians quietly call on him to bring out the black vote prior to an election. High school players at Northwestern know that, if they knock on the steel mesh security door protecting his house, McAdoo will take care of them. Standout UM Hurricanes trust he'll set them up with a little money or some food or anything else they might need to tide them over through college as they make their way to the pros.

McAdoo is a street agent, a kind of super-booster little known by the public at large yet common enough to have earned its own subspecies and genus. Almost every major college sports program has a street agent, or two, or maybe twelve. These are guys who operate under the radar, usually unseen and unknown by even the sportswriters who cover the teams. Guys who players know to hit up for a couple of dollars to get a pizza and catch a movie—or maybe buy a new car, as has been documented in some cases. Street agents—usually inner-city residents, often respected members of their community—can occasionally cause problems for a program. Players aren't supposed to receive any compensation from anyone, booster or not. A University of Michigan street agent pleaded guilty to money laundering and other charges after he showered gifts on standout Wolverine basketball player Chris Webber and others.

"McAdoo, he raised Snoop," says Maurice Robinson, the twenty-five-year-old father of five, referring to Northwestern High, FSU, and now Kansas City Chiefs wide receiver Snoop Minnis. "He raised Edgerrin James at Miami and Nate Webster and Bubba Franks. He bought them what they needed. He gave them money so they wouldn't be tempted to get things in the wrong way. McAdoo bought Snoop his first car. Ask Snoop. He did. He said to Snoop, 'If you guys win the state championship, I'll buy you a car.' And that's what they did so that's what he did.

"How does he pay for it? Out of love. I don't know the exact way he makes his money. He gives it away out of love. He supports Trina [the rising rap star from Liberty City]. He doesn't give only to football players—he gives to basketball players too. If you wasn't a good athlete he'd give to you too. He is all about love."

It's as a football booster that McAdoo is best known. He attends every Northwestern High game. He'll usually share the team's pregame dinner. Sometimes he'll bring an enormous sheet cake purchased at a Winn-Dixie supermarket, telling the team they can eat it only if they win, and they better win because he "didn't spend no fifty dollars on no cake" just to watch them lose. On the inside of his right forearm McAdoo sports a large tattoo of the orange-and-green logo of the University of Miami, underneath which is inked the word "NUT." The tattoo is for Nate Webster, the Northwestern alum who went on to shine as a college linebacker.

"We got scars alike, we got cars alike," McAdoo says of his relationship with Webster. "The '72 Cutlass out there on the street—we both have his and hers '72 Cutlasses. Ten years ago he wanted mine so bad I asked my friend to give him his."

Ten years ago Webster was a Northwestern High School freshman.

"I just love football," McAdoo continues. "I came from a family with two parents so that's all I know. Most of these guys came from a family with one parent. And ain't no father figure in their life. And I stepped in. Yeah! Kaboom! That's no secret. That's what I was with all of 'em, a father figure. EJ, Nut—with all of 'em."

🏈 🏈 🏈

McAdoo sets down his markers and pushes himself up from the counter. He seems much older than his forty-three years of age; simply lumbering barefoot across orange shag carpeting is a difficult maneuver for him. He enters his bedroom. The floor is littered with football detritus: game balls from the Pop Warner Super Bowl and from the Pop Warner city championship; five other footballs are encased in Lucite. A wall of sneakers—both Nike and Adidas—border a mattress almost to pillow level. His son's number 61 Warriors jersey lays atop of a dresser next to Nate Webster's blue-and-gold

Northwestern jersey. Also on the dresser stand stacks of bubble-gum trading cards and laminated snapshots of Northwestern alumni playing in the pros. Near the dresser, atop a yard-high pile of old programs and newspaper clippings, rests a photo album of McAdoo's trip to the NFL Pro Bowl in Hawaii, with every print autographed by the players whose images he captured.

"That's Snoop's baby momma," he says, pointing to a framed picture of an attractive young woman. "I paid for her to go to the prom. I paid for him to go to the prom with her." McAdoo moves his finger ten degrees to the left. "Over there, that's Nate Webster's baby momma. I sent her to the prom. I bought that dress for her."

On the wall hangs a poster of a young black woman wearing only a strategic covering of soap bubbles. It's Trina, the rapper closely aligned with Trick Daddy. "I raised her, you know," McAdoo says, his 1995 Northwestern Bulls state championship ring gleaming as he points to the poster. "Me and her momma went to school together. I helped out with food."

Jostling for space alongside the poster are yellow-and-black Warrior pom-poms, blue-and-gold Northwestern Bull pom-poms, and orange-and-green Miami Hurricane pom-poms. A second poster celebrates UM's defeat of Florida in the Sugar Bowl. The slats on the venetian blinds alternate 'Canes colors. Another pile of newspaper clippings climbs nearly to the ceiling.

Tiptoeing around a pair of cleats, then stepping over a yellow football helmet, McAdoo reaches a closet, which he opens to reveal his Hall of Jerseys. The first selection is green and gold, number 88. It's the Packers jersey worn by Bubba Franks, the former tight end at UM. "Number ten in the 2000 draft," McAdoo says, gingerly laying the jersey on the bed. He pulls out the number 5 jersey Edgerrin James wore at the University of Miami. A dozen other jerseys land on the bed, including the number 88 jersey worn at Northwestern by Antonio Bryant, the wide receiver at the University of Pittsburgh expected to go high in the upcoming NFL draft.

"I was helping out, pure point blank," he says, explaining his role in the lives of these star athletes. "I didn't went out and recruit nobody. The only persons I helped out was the ones that came and knocked on my door. Nobody from out of the hood. Nobody from out of the county. The only persons I helped out was the persons I know."

The desire to help kids is something that was born with him, he says. He's been doing it his whole life. Until recently, he admits, his generosity had fallen only on Liberty City's best athletes. Nate Webster wore one of McAdoo's suits on the day he signed to play for the Hurricanes.

"After he took his SATs in 1996, he came around and said he passed," McAdoo relays. "He bang on my window. 'I passed! I passed! I passed!' I asked him what his momma think and he said he hadn't even told her yet."

When Bobby Bowden, the head coach at Florida State, came down from Tallahassee to recruit Snoop Minnis, it was McAdoo that Bowden met with. "I cussed Bobby out but good," McAdoo recalls. "I tore into his ass. I wanted Snoop to go to UM."

Even though Minnis attended FSU anyway—a pretty good decision, as he was named an all-American and became a second-round pick in the 2001 NFL draft—McAdoo maintained a strong presence in the athlete's life.

"After Martin dropped out of Pop Warner we were over at McAdoo's house trying to see if there was any way to keep him in the program," recalls the Warriors' Brian Johnson. "While we were there Snoop called. And this was when he was still at FSU. Mack was yelling at him because he hadn't been attending classes or his grades were down or something. Even from where we were sitting across the room, you could tell that Snoop was hit hard. He was just saying, 'Yes, sir,' and 'No, sir.'"

● ● ●

As a kid McAdoo showed a gift for sports—his nickname is the last name of a Hall of Fame basketball forward, Bob McAdoo, with whose jump shot his once earned favorable comparisons—but there wasn't time for organized athletics. His father sold watermelons out of the back of a truck, and conscripted McAdoo's labor. Officially, McAdoo still sells watermelons for a living.

"I sell produce, but what I really got is a gift for game," he explains. "I throw bets. I'm a con artist. Whatever. I can basically talk." He pulls a torn shred of paper from the front pocket of his polyester work pants. Scribbled in ballpoint ink is a series of four-digit numbers. The paper is a receipt for an underground lottery. "I like numbers. I play with numbers for a living. I pick numbers every day."

It's hard to trace McAdoo's income. He sells watermelons and he plays the numbers. Does that generate enough money to buy cars for star athletes? McAdoo admits that his cash flow is supplemented by his relationships with some of Liberty City's more prominent entrepreneurs. The list includes some of the most notorious drug dealers to ever work Miami.

"Everybody in the neighborhood who know me know I'm down with the John Does," he says, referring to a gang believed responsible for at least a dozen drug-related executions. "Those are my boys. I watched 'em grow up. I raised 'em myself." He lifts his cell phone. "I might get a call from Mr. John Doe here any minute. [Imprisoned gang leader Corey Smith] calls me three, four times a week. He calls me to ask me to check up on his boy, just like I'd do for him. If things were switched? Boom! I'd want him to look after my boy if I couldn't. I want my boy taken care of."

This association with the John Does, however strong it may actually be (these things are difficult to verify beyond word of mouth), makes it easy to dismiss McAdoo as a criminal, or as an accessory to crimes as deep as murder. Yet in Liberty City his contacts are not viewed unfavorably. When federal authorities arrested a drug lord operating out of the predominantly black suburb of Opa-locka, residents rallied against the arrest. The dealer had opened a gym, a couple of restaurants, and a convenience store. At Thanksgiving he had distributed free turkeys.

"Don't be knocking a drug dealer just 'cause he a drug dealer," says Dre Greene, a former coach at Gwen Cherry Park. "They be buying these boys cleats. At Christmas they buy presents for these mommas because they know they boys ain't gonna be getting nothing. Don't be knocking them at all."

McAdoo maintains a fierce allegiance to the football program at Northwestern, the high school he first attended. (He graduated from a school in South Carolina, where his family had temporarily moved.) Not only did his love for the Bulls inspire him to buy cars and prom tuxedos for the team's star players, it's also the reason why his son Martin was conceived in the first place.

"I asked his momma in '88 no, '87—I said, 'I want to have a boy to play for Northwestern," McAdoo recollects. 'You have that boy and you can leave out of my life.' All I dreamed of was to have a boy to play for Northwestern. All these years, you know what I mean?"

Martin Wright is a seventh grader now. He's heavy enough—and more than talented enough—to play for the 145-pound team at Hadley Park. He isn't playing, though. He hasn't played football in three years. He still can't read, and because he can't read his mother won't let him play. When McAdoo saw his son's bad grades derail any dreams of football glory, he changed the focus of his boosterism. No longer is he all about gridiron excellence. Now he is completely, almost obsessively focused on education.

McAdoo formed an underground charitable corporation, unregistered with the state, the capital behind it rather sketchy. He calls the foundation by the acronym REAL: Read and Educate Athletes for Life. As the head of REAL, McAdoo crafts thank-you cards for coaches and for administrators such as Sam Johnson at Hadley Park. He brings public speakers to practices to remind boys to stay in school. He convinced the Edgerrin James Charitable Foundation to distribute thirty-two bicycles to honor roll students throughout the county. Thirty-two is Edgerrin James's number with the Colts. Next year McAdoo hopes to increase the number of bikes distributed by securing funding from the Packers' Bubba Franks, who wears number 88.

"This whole thing started basically with my son," he explains. "I figured that he was set because he was all–Pop Warner, but he had no grades. He wasn't getting his academics right. So, boom! That's where it started from, right then. I want to help my son, but I want to help other kids too. Blacks own football in Dade County. We own it! But we ain't going nowhere without education, bottom line. You lack the education, it's jail."

Some of the funding for the organization, McAdoo admits, comes from unnamed local businessmen. Much of the money comes from Edgerrin James, who grew up in Immokalee, a rural town where McAdoo's father bought his watermelons. McAdoo convinced James to sponsor a scholarship program for thirty-two kids each at three different parks, a total of ninety-six kids. Each kid is selected on the basis of his grades, not for his play on the field. Each is monitored year-round, not just during football season. Good report cards win T-shirts and tickets to Dolphin games. Down the line, McAdoo hopes to see two or three kids from each park receive scholarship money to college. He dreams of expanding the program into every park in the county.

"Boom!" he shouts. "This thing right here is the biggest thing happening in Dade County."

Probably not. Despite some obviously positive aspects to his program, McAdoo's efforts are often viewed with amusement. His homemade posters, like the one he's drafting for Sam today, wouldn't ribbon at an elementary school biennial. The speakers he procures—usually firemen and police officers—are solid citizens, but their careers and their advice to stay in school fail to capture the attention of the average fourth grader, much less one from Liberty City.

"McAdoo, he just a . . . a groupie type," says Tangela Stanley, the assistant cheerleading coordinator at Hadley Park. "He just hanging on them, on EJ and them. But he has changed. He is more positive now, he is; I'll give him that. He's doing the right thing now. He trying."

Whatever anyone might think of McAdoo's REAL program, there's no denying his commitment, nor his good intentions. He visits at least one park almost every day. He hands out plaques seemingly at random. Just about every night he's back at his kitchen counter stenciling new posters.

"Check this out," he commands. "Soon as I get my life right from cursing and the drinking the beer and stuff, I'm going to get behind the pulpit. I'm here for a purpose. And I would be wrong if I don't share it with these kids. I'm here for a purpose. I know I can really help the community and help kids. I know that. I got the power and I got the juice and I got the swagger and I got the NFL players, right? People listen. And this community needs me."

Chapter 9

Liberty City at Palmetto

Less than forty years ago, Miami was as segregated as any city in the Deep South. Palmetto, one of its better suburbs, remains close enough to its roots that a pickup truck flying a rebel flag gets no double takes. Parents move into the houses across from Palmetto Field so their kids can attend Miami's best public schools. The rugby team that practices at the field on Tuesday and Thursday nights is mostly white and prosperous, like Palmetto itself.

Yet tonight, as on all football nights, the field is populated almost exclusively by blacks. Many of the players walked over from the housing projects on the west side of Dixie Highway, a place where the schools aren't so desirable and where the poverty rate hovers above 20 percent.

Near the berm that separates the practice field from a grocery store parking lot, Palmetto Raiders head coach Raul Campos introduces his offense to the plan for the home game Saturday against Liberty City. Campos stands the players in formation as if they were chess pieces, then instructs them on exactly where to run when the ball is snapped. Campos drafts his game plan on Sunday night. On Tuesday, the first practice day of the week, he presents the plan to the team. By the end of practice today, Friday, every play has been run and rerun so many times it is embedded in his players' muscle memories.

"Ain't going to teach nothing to no one on Saturday," Campos says as he watches a play unfold. He's still dressed for summer, in a white polo shirt embroidered with the logo of the Pop Warner Super Bowl 2000. A whistle tickles his chest. "By Saturday you've just got to line 'em up."

On the practice field, there is no joking around. No one is smiling. At the line of scrimmage, the quarterback—who's been working with Campos for three years and who knows the system as well as anyone—shifts a wide receiver into the proper position. A fast prospect with the nickname Nightmare is told to run a few plays. He seamlessly moves into the lineup as another wide receiver steps out. Raider practices are efficient and professional. They're also as boring as roadwork in advance of a marathon run.

In their last game the Raiders shut out Inner City by 24 points. To reward their performance, Campos invited several of his players to spend an afternoon with him at a construction site. (It was a teacher workday, so there was no school.) He paid each player $20 for what he calls, "forty-five minutes of bullshit work." One of those players not invited to the site shows up late for practice. He stands atop the berm slowly pulling a red jersey over his shoulder pads.

"Come on, Carl, let's go," Campos calls out to him. "You don't make a living up there, you make a living down here on the football field. Let's go. Loosen up."

🏈 🏈 🏈

For the 95-pound Warriors from Liberty City, it wasn't supposed to play out like this: a record of 1–3 and a real danger of missing the playoffs. It was supposed to be another march to the city championship, then on to Orlando and a week at Disney World. Magic. Space Mountain and Mickey Mouse and a second national championship. "If You Believe It You Can Achieve It" announced the banner at practice that first day back in July. What we believe, Coach Brian Johnson told his recruits as they stood in the sun with dust on their cleats and sweat rushing down their small, smooth faces, is that the Warriors are going all the way. We will win the Super Bowl. We've done it before.

Yet now, in late September, on the hour-long bus ride down Dixie Highway, Johnson is calculating the slim odds of salvaging the season. A one-touchdown loss to Goulds. A one-touchdown loss to Overtown. A two-touchdown loss to lowly Florida City, a team that hasn't yet won another game. The Warriors' only win came via forfeit after the opposition simply failed to show up. Brian drags a hand over his round, shaved head.

"I've never lost this way," he says with an equal mixture of anger and puzzlement, the American flags of a passing used car dealership reflecting in his eyeglasses. "Every year we won. Every year. I mean, we . . . never . . . lost. It's hard for me to understand."

Even as the losses mount, however, there is reason for hope. Practice went well this week. Phillip Thomas stepped up at running back, crashing through defenders with the ferocity that everyone expects from him. In an attempt to capitalize on Phillip's emerging potential, Brian stripped the fancy offense down to just a few basic running plays. A secondary benefit to the changes: Quarterback Antwane almost never runs in the wrong direction anymore. Things may be coming together, finally, and just in time. If the season is to be saved it's going to have to start tonight with a win over Palmetto—undefeated Palmetto, at the 95-pound level the best team in the league.

"This is the upset tonight," guarantees an assistant coach as the Warriors pour off the bus at Palmetto Field. "We know what we have to do. We'll stay focused."

The lights at Palmetto Field are already ablaze. The 85s play out the undercard as fans tailgate on lawn chairs beyond the west end zone. A crew of young men lean against the west goalpost, their eyelids as droopy as their shorts. Girls in tube-top dresses parade toward the bleachers. Raul Campos sits on an overturned milk crate eating chicken and yellow rice. His team of teenagers will play the Warrior 145s tomorrow afternoon. He's not the least bit worried.

"We had a real good practice today," he says, a grain of rice shooting from his mouth toward the goalpost. "Real good. Everybody looked sharp. We executed well. We looked real good."

The Liberty City 95s gather in the shadows behind the visitors' bleachers. They strap on their plastic shoulder pads and wind laps of duct tape around their waists to hold up their pants. Tiny hands grab torn "away" jerseys, white with black numbers.

"We gonna win," insists Brandon, a safety.

"We gonna win," echoes Chase, a receiver.

Stevie, the Deion Sanders acolyte, postures confidently. "Palmetto, they look hard but they really soft," he says. "We will stop 'em on every play."

Phillip is his usual taciturn self: "I feel good. I'm ready to play some football."

There is a reassuring energy, a vibe from the strong practices mixed with an electricity that comes only on Friday night under the lights. The confidence appears to have turned. With their pants secure and their jerseys tucked in, the Warriors break into groups for instruction from their position coaches. Head coach Brian walks from one huddle to the next, monitoring the lessons.

". . . We not gonna win the game if you don't go out and block hard," says Beasley, the offensive coordinator. He sits on a milk crate to address seven members of his backfield. "They already expect you to lose, and that's good, that mean they not ready for y'all. . . ."

". . . Jajuan, if you make a tackle, let me know. I want to hear you whoop it up, all right?" pleads Coach Chico, the defensive assistant. He wants his four linebackers to make more noise during games. "We gonna go with DaQuan and Kevin at the tackles. Gotta go fast, gotta get in and hit. Gotta get out there and knock 'em around. No fear! It's do or die tonight. . . ."

" . . . Get centered!" barks offensive line coach Ed. "Face up— let's go! Stutter-step at me now. *Stop* that choppy step; if you gonna run, run. Terrance! Put on your game face! Right here, now, right in the middle. If you keep your hands right here at the groin you gonna stop 'em. . . ."

". . . This is the upset tonight," defensive coordinator coach Pete assures the cornerbacks. "We know what we have to do. We gonna stay focused."

Brian blows into his whistle.

"Bring it in!" he roars. "Right now! It's time!" A bouquet of yellow helmets blooms around his waist. Immediately following last week's loss to Overtown, four parents demanded that Brian be replaced at head coach by someone more experienced, by someone who can deliver the wins they've come to expect. Brian insists he's immune to the pressure. It's just football, he says. Yet here, minutes before kickoff, the bulging veins on his neck reveal the stress he is under.

"I want you to go out and kick them in their fucking balls!" he commands. "You do that we win this game. Each and every one of you gonna win. You be there, we win the game. They get the ball, what we gonna do?"

"Kill 'em!" replies Ruben, a reserve.

"We gonna knock 'em out!" Brian clarifies. "They get the ball we knock 'em out. Fight hard! Be Warriors!"

Palms slap padded thighs. Stevie leads the team in call and response.

> Su Womp Womp!
> *Su Womp Womp!*
> Sugar Rang Atang!
> *Sugar Rang Atang!*
> The Warriors run this thang!
> *The Warriors run this thang!*

Clap. Clap. Slap.

> Ninety-five!
> *Ninety-five!*
> Don't take no jive!
> *Don't take no jive!*

Lost three games!
Lost three games!
It ain't no shame!
It ain't no shame!
Doin' good!
Doin' good!
Just like we should!
Just like we should!
Now hit those pads!

Clap. Clap. Slap.

The players dash toward the end zone, mobilizing into a platoon. To the office workers driving home in their SUVs and sedans, Palmetto Field probably looks like nothing special: a few hundred people on dimly lit turf, two sets of rickety bleachers, a haze of barbecue smoke. The Warriors, they know what's on the line. Cleats bounce on the turf. Players bang face masks. Fists pound shoulder pads.

"Let's get ready, boys," shouts an assistant coach. "Show me something!"

Who you gonna beat?
Palmetto!

What time is it?
Showtime!
Showtime!
Showtime!

🏈 🏈 🏈

The score at halftime is 21–0. The Warriors are not winning.

"Let's get in the game, y'all. This is embarrassing," cries Coach Chico, dragging a cooler of water over to where the Warriors sit with bowed heads.

"That's the whole team problem," Coach Pete adds. "Too much negativity. 'Warrior Pride' don't mean you have an undefeated team. 'Warrior Pride' means when you face adversity you reach deep inside you and you face it. We didn't come all the way down here to see you play like this. Y'all gotta play ball!"

The game ended, effectively, on the opening kickoff. Only ten Warriors took to the field. Parents in the bleachers called out to Brian to add the requisite eleventh player. Brian, perhaps stunned that his game plan had derailed before the clock even started ticking, couldn't figure out who was missing. On the Warriors' opening offensive play, a simple handoff, a Palmetto linebacker crushed Phillip so brutally the runner lay on his back for a full minute, trying to wheeze air back into his lungs. Palmetto's offense, in contrast, scored on each of its first three drives.

A father pulls Brian aside. "Coach, I don't mean to disrespect you," the father says, "but y'all gotta get out there and kick ass. Kick ass, y'all."

Late in the second half, with the clock running and the score climbing beyond reach, another Warrior goes down. Number 77, linebacker Warren Baynoe, collapses at the 35-yard line. He slumps on his left shoulder, his eyes blinking and open.

"He's talking, right?" asks Coach Pete, the first out on the field. The rest of the coaches join Pete in a scrum over Warren's motionless body.

"Yeah, he's talking," Brian says, lightly shaking Warren's shoulder. It's probably a neck injury. Although it doesn't look serious, an ambulance is summoned. Warren's cousin, a teammate on the Warriors, pokes his head inside the huddle of coaches.

"Is he dead?" the cousin asks.

The ambulance, bumping across Palmetto Field's uneven turf, jostles Warren a bit. He squirms, not so much in pain as in recognition that he's in an ambulance, on a stretcher, and has license to act mortally wounded. Brian grasps Warren's small hand. The Warriors' head coach stares out the rectangular rear windows at the field, watching his players shrink in size. When the ambulance turns onto the street, Palmetto Field, and the loss to the Raiders, fades from sight.

How in the world did it all go this bad? Brian's never lost before. Not when he was coaching the 65-pounders, not when he served as an assistant on the 95s. One of those teams even won a national title. But at this point in this season, after this loss, even making the playoffs appears unlikely. That trip to Orlando he'd spent all off-season dreaming about? Forget it. Or better yet, given his mood, fuck it. Fuck everything.

"I'm pullin' shit out of my ass," Brian says, searching for an explanation. "I mean, trying to figure out what the *fuck* is wrong. Are they that much more talented than us? Is that all it is?"

The ambulance pulls up to suburban Baptist Hospital. Brian walks beside the stretcher, through the lobby, into the emergency room. His wife, who followed in their car, heads for the waiting room.

When Warren had collapsed on the field, Brian had tried to reach the boy's mother on his cell phone. No one ever answered. Warren has no father to speak of, and none of his other relatives bothered to attend the game. Even finding someone at home on a Friday night proved to be a challenge. Only hours after the game ended, when Brian finally located a cousin, was he told that Warren's mother would come to the hospital to retrieve her son. But when? On the TV in the lobby, the news is over, Letterman is done, and now Conan is surrendering the airwaves to some talk show Brian has never seen before. With Warren stabilized—it's just a sprain—Brian slumps into a hard blue plastic chair and tries again to reach the mother.

"I don't know why I even bother," he says, mostly to himself. Why spend three hours a day, five days a week teaching somebody else's kids? He could be at home watching TV or playing around on his computer. He could spend more time with his own kids. He's not doing it for the money, that's for sure. And as for the boys, well, they're plain sorry. Antwane can't complete a pass to save his life.

Phillip's a puzzle. Brandon's father coaches from the bleachers. At least Brandon has a father; most of the boys don't. One need look no further than Warren for proof of that.

At close to 1:30 A.M., the sliding electronic doors to the emergency room swish open. Warren's mother stumbles in. She's wearing spandex hot pants that fail to cover the full flesh of her buttocks. In her left hand she holds car keys. In her right hand she holds a plastic cup radiating Wild Turkey fumes. Brian stares in her direction, at her outfit, at the bourbon.

"Man," he says to his wife, speaking softly to not be overheard. "Some of these boys, their lives are a living hell."

Chapter 10

Plex

Blue Lake Point, an apartment complex north of Miami, looks like a roadside hotel you'd never want to sleep in. Identical three-story buildings extend in a line ten blocks long. The steel doors of every apartment open onto the speeding cars and trucks of Northwest 103rd Street. Toddlers climb concrete stairs dented with holes wide enough for them to fall through. A barbed-wire fence protects the mailboxes. Spray-paint signatures personalize the exterior walls.

On May 18, 1995, a four-door Nissan Altima idled in park in the lot outside Blue Lake Point. Behind the wheel sat Otis Green, age twenty-eight. His on-again, off-again girlfriend, Alice Mae Gardner, age thirty-seven, sat in the passenger seat. In the back sat a friend, Brian Gibson, age twenty-two. On Gardner's lap sat her son, Michael Frazier. The ambush took place at ten in the morning.

The three adults were debating where they were going to eat lunch when another car suddenly pulled up alongside them. According to Gibson, there were several people in the second car, though it was hard to tell exactly how many because the car's windows were tinted deep black. Two of those windows rolled down. At least two men leaned out, both armed with AK-47s, or what the police would later describe as "assault-type weapons."

By the time detectives arrived at Blue Lake Point, more than twenty-five bullet casings littered the parking lot. Although the assassination took place at midday outside an apartment complex in which hundreds of people live, detectives failed to find a single witness to the crime.

"They were not getting a great deal of cooperation," a police spokesman said. "They had difficulty getting the most routine questions answered."

Green, the driver of the Nissan, died instantly in the hail of bullets. Gardner died later that night. Gibson, in the backseat, survived a serious wounding. Michael Frazier wasn't as lucky. One of the bullets pierced the hard bone of his cranium and lodged in his brain. He lived long enough to be transported to the Jackson Hospital trauma unit, where he was initially listed in worse-than-critical condition. Two days later he died. He was five years old.

● ● ●

The riots of the eighties devastated Liberty City. Almost as soon as the last Dumpster fire died, most large manufacturers fled for safer quarters. The Norton Tire Company, for example, moved its headquarters and its steady supply of good jobs to the suburbs. Efforts to revive Liberty City's economy floundered. One program to provide loans for black businesses channeled money instead primarily to Hispanics. In the employment vacuum, Liberty City fell under the control of rival drug gangs. Seven major outfits worked the streets, along with countless smaller crews. The two largest gangs were the John Does, so-called because they didn't have a formal nickname, and the Boobie Boys.

Both gangs moved tons of cocaine through Miami. Each set up business partnerships with suppliers in Latin America. Franchised distribution networks spread throughout the Southeast. To protect the drug holes they controlled near Hadley Park, John Doe lieutenants committed at least five murders that were discussed on phones tapped by police. One shoot-out took place at a gas station in broad daylight. Three drug dealers in Overtown were shot at high noon by assassins so bloodthirsty they didn't bother to roll down their car windows before firing.

"It used to be pretty bad," recalls the Warriors' Brian Johnson, who grew up on the same block as the leader of the John Does. "When it started you'd hear about someone getting shot and you'd say, 'Man, wow, someone got shot.' After a while, when gunshots went off and another person went down, it was, like, not even news."

The gang presence affected football in Liberty City. When the John Does expressed their displeasure with the head coach at Northwestern High, the coach immediately transferred to lesser rival Central High. It was nothing for a Boobie Boy or a John Doe to drop a $10,000 bet on his favorite team. And not only at the high school level, but in Pop Warner as well.

"Back in the national championship year, we still had the John Doe gang running around the park," recalls Daryl Hence, the former head coach of the Warrior 95s who now oversees the football program. "Now, I don't know them from anyone, but they was out here scouting our practices and such. Our first game of the season was against Overtown. When we got to their field this guy who had been watching us practice was over there too. And he knew what we were up to. He bet someone over there a thousand dollars that we would score on the opening kickoff.

"We score a touchdown and go up 7–0. We come right back and stop them, which means we get the ball back. This guy, he offers his friend an even richer bet. It's now three thousand dollars that on the first play from scrimmage we score again. The guy takes the bet and we run a 24-power, a play that usually scored for us. And that time, like he bet, it did score. We lost the game 14–13, but he comes over afterward and says, 'Coach, I just won four grand and I want to spread it around the kids.'

"I told him, 'No, bro. I don't roll like that. If you want to give it to the kids, I won't let you, unless it's your kid.' That's dope money. That's all it was. Four thousand dollars is like pocket change to him. It'd be like me buying a dollar scratch-off lottery ticket, that's how little it was to him."

Despite Daryl's efforts to protect his kids, the gang presence infiltrated the team, sometimes in obvious ways. The great Martin

Wright, the then-nine-year-old dynamo who anchored the War-riors' national championship team, wore jersey number 61 for a reason.

"That's 'cause he's down with the John Does," says McAdoo, his father. "He's representing 61st Street. That's where the John Does are from. That's my street. He's representing for the John Does."

🏈 🏈 🏈

When Diamond Pless is asked about the best day of his life, he doesn't need more than a second to recall it.

"The best day of my life was the day when I first saw football," he says, his narrow eyes wider than usual, his squeaky voice flow-ing so fast he sounds like a cassette tape caught half on play and half on fast-forward. "It was on this game—at that time we had a PlayStation—and *Madden NFL Football* was on. So I saw that and I was like, 'Hey, Dad, what's that you're playing?' And he said, 'Foot-ball!' And I was like, 'Can I play?' So he showed me how to play it, showed me what buttons to press to win and all that. I started mess-ing up at first so I used to play every day. And then I started getting good and, so, I was like, 'Football rules!'

"I liked playing it so much on the PlayStation I asked if I could play it for real. He says, 'Yeah, you can play it.' He said, 'In about two years you're going to be able to play it.' And then I just waited. And I waited. Now can I play it."

Diamond never knew his birth father. According to Diamond's uncle Durell, the birth father was a fantastic athlete, a star at North-western High, someone whose name would be recognized by any fan of Miami high school sports. He was known on the football field for his speed, a gift he used to run from Shakitha as soon as she be-came pregnant with Diamond. By the time of Diamond's birth, in 1991, Shakitha had hooked up with a new man. His name was Arthur Clarence Pless II. He was eighteen years old on the day Diamond was born. The boy took his last name. Arthur Pless be-came Diamond's legal father.

Arthur Pless, or "Plex" as everybody calls him, had played football himself, also at Northwestern High. In the summer and on weekends he'd invite Diamond over to his house in northwest Dade. In the backyard, Diamond, along with Plex's four other sons, drilled on plays and formations. It was in that backyard that Diamond first learned how to tackle. Diamond wears jersey number 33 for the Warriors, the same number his father wore in high school.

"He was so serious about football," Durell says of Plex. "He would have them in the backyard hitting early in the morning. He did it, like, a lot more intense than me. When they messed up he'd have them stand out there like this"—Durell extends his arms wide—"spread Jesus in full gear, and the other kids would clobber 'em."

Plex never lived with Diamond and Shakitha, but he would come over frequently to watch TV or play video games. When he was watching a game, and when the broadcast broke away to commercials, he'd sometimes show Diamond his tattoos, of which there were too many for Diamond to count. One was an enormous cross inked on his back. A skeleton danced on his left arm.

Plex's first documented arrest occurred in 1993. It was a misdemeanor, for obstructing a police officer. Later that year he was pulled over because the plates on his scooter had expired. During the traffic stop, officers retrieved from his left front pocket a bag containing cocaine. In his right front pocket Plex had stashed a folded wad adding up to $550. He received probation for narcotics possession. He consistently failed to meet with his parole officer, who filed a petition recommending his probation be revoked. Within a year, Plex managed to be arrested again, for misdemeanor assault and battery.

There are other county and city charges, all in the same vein. If they were the extent of it, Plex would be nothing more than a petty, if career, criminal, a guy caught up in a common Liberty City life of small-time drug dealing.

"He made money in drugs, but in my opinion, drugs were a fact of life here," says Durell, a former drug dealer himself. "You made your money, you got caught, you did your time. At least, that's the way it was until all those people started getting killed—innocent people like kids and such."

In the early 1990s, a drug dealer named Kenneth "Boobie" Williams established himself as the primary distributor of crack cocaine in Miami. Working in partnership with the Brown twins—one named Leonard, the other Lenard—Williams converted cocaine he obtained from contacts in Colombia and Panama into crack. The conversion occurred at a laboratory set up in the house of the Brown twins' mother. The Silver Blue Lake apartments became a distribution center. After it was processed in Miami, couriers transported the crack to associates in north Florida, Georgia, South Carolina, and elsewhere.

To maintain and protect the distribution network, its operators shed blood. A lot of blood. At least fifteen murders have been officially linked to the Boobie Boys, some in gangland style. Police believe the Boys may have murdered as many as thirty-five people and initiated up to a hundred drive-by shootings. On February 24, 1999, two months before Diamond turned eight years old, Arthur "Plex" Pless was charged in federal court with six of the Boobie Boys murders, along with possession and distribution of cocaine.

The night before he turned himself in, Plex stayed at Shakitha's apartment in Miami. He watched a San Francisco 49ers game with Diamond. Plex was smiling and laughing and in a good mood, Diamond recalls, as if it was a normal Sunday night, as if he wasn't worried about anything. When Diamond woke up the next morning, his father had already left for the police station, where he approached the duty agent and said, "I'm wanted." At his arraignment Plex pleaded not guilty to all the charges.

The trial of the Boobie Boys was at that time the biggest drug trial in the history of a state familiar with drug crimes. Plex was just one of sixteen defendants, but his was among the more difficult cases for his lawyers to defend. One witness testified that Plex admitted to murdering Everett Cooper, a rival drug dealer. Another witness claimed in court that Plex had hired him to assassinate Johnny Beliard, with whom Plex was embroiled in a drug-turf dispute. Both witnesses testified that Plex had admitted his role in the murder of a man named Roosevelt Wing. Additionally, according to documents on file at the federal courthouse:

"Det. Sgt. David Simmons of the Miami-Dade Police Department testified that Pless procured fifteen-year-old Anthony Brandey to drive the car used to murder victims Otis Green, Alice Gardner, and Michael Frazier at the [Blue Lake Point] apartment complex. Detective Simmons relayed that according to Brandey, Pless and co-defendant Ben Johnson donned ski masks and murdered the three victims in an effort to eradicate Green as a rival drug dealer in the area. Brian Gibson, who survived the shooting, stated that he heard Pless state, 'Otis had to go.'"

The trial lasted six weeks. Diamond went to the courtroom only once. He sat in the gallery that day fidgeting on an uncomfortably hard wooden bench. His father turned around and smiled to let him know everything was fine. Then the jury foreman read the verdict. And prosecutors celebrated the defeat of the largest drug conspiracy ring in U.S. history.

Kenneth "Boobie" Williams received five concurrent life sentences. One of the Brown twins died in prison of a heart attack before trial. His brother will also die in prison, having received two life sentences without the possibility of parole. Only one of the sixteen people arrested in the sweep was cleared of all charges. The rest received sentences ranging from sixty months in prison to life. A former Miami-Dade police officer was sentenced to more than fifteen years for using his patrol car to steal drugs and cash from rival drug dealers.

The jury found Plex guilty of three of the eight counts he faced: cocaine possession, distribution, and using a machine gun to perpetrate a drug crime. Federal Judge K. Michael Moore sentenced Plex to two concurrent life sentences, plus, for the gun count, an additional two hundred and forty months in prison. Plex can never be paroled.

The conviction of the Boobie Boys was just one of the drug-related successes the U.S. Attorney's Office enjoyed in the late 1990s.

The John Does were also functionally dismantled, as were several smaller outfits. Since the arrests and convictions, the murder rate in Liberty City has dropped by more than half.

Plex is serving his time at a federal prison in Terre Haute, Indiana. Once a week, usually on Saturdays, he calls Diamond to talk.

"He asks about my football," Diamond reports. "I ask him if he's eating healthy." Plex never talks about why he's in jail. Diamond writes his father a letter every two weeks or so. "I ask him if he's losing weight. I answer the questions he asks me over the phone and in his letters. He wants to know how I'm doing in school. He wants to know how I'm doing in football."

Chapter 11

Election

One day after Palmetto effectively ended the 95-pound Warriors' season, the older boys on Raul Campos's Raiders administered a similar execution of Liberty City's 145-pounders. Playing on a dusty field worn from hosting two days of games, the Raiders scored seemingly at will.

"It's working just like we drew it up," Campos said at halftime. He pointed to the bleachers and to a group of teenage boys in matching blue T-shirts and shorts. It was the Richmond squad that beat the Raiders earlier in the year. "Look at them," Campos sneered. "Why would they bring their whole team and all of their coaching staff if we weren't in their heads. That's where we want to be—in their heads."

The following Saturday, Campos chartered a motor coach so his Raiders could ride in air-conditioned comfort to Overtown and an away game against the Rattlers. Overtown, originally Nigger Town, was once an epicenter of black culture. Cab Calloway and Billie Holiday played Overtown's clubs. Though boxer Muhammad Ali trained for his first heavyweight championship fight on Miami Beach, he slept in an Overtown hotel. The spires of dozens of black churches formed a skyline on 14th Street.

In 1971, when construction of I-95 carved the heart out of Overtown, most blacks relocated to Liberty City. What's left is an almost clichéd assembly of package stores and crumbling apartment buildings. Overtown's Pop Warner program, which formed soon after the Warriors revived black football, is one of the decimated community's brightest lights. The Rattlers wear orange helmets with white letters spelling out "Towners 4 Life" affixed to one side.

Interest in Overtown's game against Coach Campos is so strong that the most popular urban radio station in town, 99 Jamz, has plugged the contest all week long.

"I like, 'Holy shit! I ain't never heard *that* before,'" one Raiders player tells a teammate as their bus motors into Overtown. "I ain't never heard us mentioned on the radio before."

On Thanksgiving 1999, two recreational fishermen found a Cuban boy named Elián Gonzalez floating on an inner tube off the coast of Pompano Beach, just north of Fort Lauderdale in Broward County. The five-year-old had left the costal town of Cárdenas on a small boat. Twelve other people accompanied him, including his mother and her boyfriend, a reputed smuggler of immigrants. The mother, the boyfriend, and eight other passengers drowned during the ninety-mile journey across the Florida Straits. When Elián was found, dehydrated, scared, and alone, he'd been adrift for as long as three days.

As anyone who watched CNN during the months that followed knows, Elián's Miami relatives took him into their Little Havana home. They enrolled him in a private school as idealistically far to the right as Cuba is to the left. They showered him with a Super Soaker squirt gun, a go-cart, a jungle gym, a puppy, and a new bunny rabbit. In countless televised interviews, they argued it would be child abuse to send Elián back to Cuba, where, in a particularly sticky development, the boy's father continued to live happily, and demanded that his son be returned to him.

In response to the father's custody request, the Miami relatives let the young refugee become the poster boy of Miami's anti-Castro exile cause. His uncles and cousins marched him before a growing number of television cameras. Cuban-American luminaries such as singer Gloria Estefan and the actor Andy Garcia paid visits. At the post-Christmas Three Kings parade down Calle Ocho, Elián sat in the bleachers surrounded by a phalanx of police officers. Parade grand marshal Orlando "El Duque" Hernandez stopped his float to climb the bleachers and give the boy a hug.

"Elián, friend, Miami is with you," the baseball pitcher told him.

As months went by, and as the custody fight escalated, extremists in Miami's exile community canonized Elián as a saint, a modern-day Christ child delivered to set Cuba free. Artists painted murals featuring scenes of Elián at sea, his inner tube protected from capsizing by the Virgin Mary (and by a trio of dolphins in her employ). The particularly devout quit their jobs to camp outside Elián's temporary home. The symbolic importance of Elián grew so potent that, even if the strong religious overtones had somehow been stripped away, the rhetoric surrounding the boy would have remained grotesquely high. One billboard in Little Havana compared Castro to both Joseph Stalin and Adolf Hitler. Cuba might as well have been Auschwitz.

On Easter Saturday 2000, armed government agents at the command of the U.S. attorney general, Janet Reno, forcefully removed Elián from his relatives' home. Cuban-Americans rioted on Flagler Street, a main thoroughfare bisecting Little Havana. Tow truck windows were smashed. Tires and Dumpsters were set ablaze. Cops faced the demonstrators shielded in full riot gear. By the time the tear gas dispersed, the racial fault lines that had long scarred Miami lay open for the rest of the world to see.

🏈 🏈 🏈

Jimmie Brown is a black pastor and the host of *Hot Talk,* a radio show broadcast Sunday nights on 99 Jamz. His program, which has aired since the 1989 Liberty City riots, was created to give Miami's blacks a place to speak their minds. During the months Elián lived in Miami, as the sides polarized, black anger toward the Cuban community dominated Brown's show. Cubans were blamed for the lack of affordable housing, the dearth of jobs, and almost any other problem blacks faced. Callers felt Cubans received too much favoritism. Why was it, they wondered, that any Cuban rafter who set foot on a Florida beach was allowed to stay in the country while any dark-skinned Haitian who made a similar voyage was repatriated?

One night a brave Cuban-American offered a dissenting opinion. Brown lost his cool.

"A caller calls up and says I wouldn't understand, that Cuba is a Third World country," he recalls. "I said, 'Girl, what 'chu talkin' about? I'm a black man in America. I know exactly what it's like to be in a Third World country.' How you gonna call a predominantly black radio station and tell me that Cubans are in slavery?"

When he's not on the radio, Brown is the pastor of Ebenezer United Methodist Church, located about a mile south of Hadley Park. Ebenezer, with its seven-story bell tower soaring over Alla-pattah, is considered the Notre Dame cathedral of black churches in Miami. The congregation, which predates the city itself, was founded in Overtown. After the construction of I-95, Ebenezer moved to its current home in what has become a Dominican community. On Sundays during service, houses surrounding the church tithe snippets of salsa music into the street.

"As a young boy, Miamuh was a great place to me," recalls retired grocer Tim Smith, age sixty-nine, an elder at Ebenezer. Smith moved to Overtown in 1946 to find work that wasn't available in his hometown on the Georgia border. After nearly six decades in Miami he continues to pronounce the city's name in the old cracker style. "We were still segregated at that time. We used the back door, the rear of any establishment. We weren't allowed to eat in a restaurant. But we had our own business areas, with nightclubs and hotels. And you'd got more places for young people to go to during those times. We had three theaters in Miamuh alone and one in Liberty City. And the floor shows were better than Las Vegas! I used to see Ray Charles for fifty cents at the Palm. Fats Domino I saw for fifty cents. All your famous stars were there—Louis Armstrong, all of them."

Of the races and nationalities that make up Miami, African-Americans are the most rooted. On Sunday afternoons, the pews at

Ebenezer are occupied by fourth- and fifth-generation Miamians. Yet in the past decade 13 percent of Miami-Dade's black population has moved out of the county. Attendance at Ebenezer is a tenth of what it was just twenty years ago. Much of the congregation that remains commutes from Pembroke Pines and Miramar, in Broward County.

When he was still a teenager, Tim Smith began working for the now-defunct Food Fair supermarket chain. In time he rose to become the only black manager in the company. He often earned assignments in the poorest-performing stores in Miami, in white neighborhoods and black. Through "hard work and preparation," he says, he was able to turn around most of the stores, usually earning himself the reward of an even worse assignment. In 1980 Smith managed a store in Liberty City. There were advantages to being a local.

"When the riot came, every store in the area was destroyed and burned up," he recalls. "I had three trailers in my back room loaded with groceries, and a meat cooler loaded with meat. People never went in my back room. No one touched the meat. I had three hundred thousand dollars in my safe and no one ever tried to roll it out of the store. Nobody even tried to take my gun."

Smith doesn't believe a young black man in Miami today has as much chance to advance professionally as he enjoyed. And as he sees it, however rooted black Miamians may be by nature, these economic realties are taking a toll.

"The black community, it's changed for the younger peoples," Smith says. "They still feel that they not getting a fair shake of opportunities that, going back years, people like me used to have. I have a cousin in the teaching profession who is now moving to Atlanta. The pressure in Atlanta is not as great as the pressure here, being a teacher. And with more money and with more benefits, that's why she's leaving.

"One of my sons, Tony, he refuse to come back to Miamuh because the opportunity just isn't there for him. The potential wasn't what he was looking for. Business opportunities for the young black are not promising here in the Miamuh area. That's why a lot of them go move out when they get married. That's what happened with my kids. And I know other kids, that's why they leave.

"I wouldn't have come to Miamuh myself if it was like this in 1946."

Not all blacks are as pessimistic as Smith. But even those who are working to improve Miami recognize the truth in Smith's words. Richard Dunn served as a Miami city commissioner in the late 1990s. A preacher, he now runs a nonprofit business aiming to build new, affordable homes in Liberty City. Like Smith, Dunn is old enough to recall the days when Overtown was a black Mecca more attractive and renowned than Atlanta. Even in segregation, Miami never suffered a real racial crisis, he says. There was no talk of hangings or lynchings. Although the Ku Klux Klan agitated when Liberty Square busted out to form Liberty City, there was never a Bull Connor fanning racial hatred.

"I'll put this out for what it's worth: The influx of Cubans is what hurt us," Dunn says. "The gains the blacks were on their way to receiving were taken away. I say that that's where a lot of the resentment comes from.

"Being black in Miami is almost—not quite, but almost—like it was being black in the fifties and the sixties in America. We have second-class citizenship. Limited opportunities. Segregation in certain tiers of life, segregation in government. A lot of blacks don't see a place where they fit in down here."

Elián returned to Cuba, where he lives a life far removed from the television cameras he endured in Miami. His house in Little Havana is now a museum, free and open to the public on Sundays. Uncle Delphin Gonzalez is usually there. He's happy to show off the bed on which Elián slept, the brush Marisleysis used to style her long brown hair, and the closet where "fisherman" Donato Dalrymple stashed Elián during the government raid.

The museum is hardly Elián's only legacy. Dalrymple remains an icon in Little Havana, cheered at parades much as Elián himself once was. Janet Reno, a Miami native who served as Miami's state attorney, has been recast, depending on one's perspective, as either a hero or the devil incarnate. Talk that she might run for governor highlights Miami's still sharp ethnic rift: The black community wants her to run and defeat incumbent governor Jeb Bush. The Cuban community pickets her house.

Among those who benefited most from Elián politics is an attorney named Manny Diaz. Although he was virtually unknown before Elián arrived, and although he has never held political office—he hadn't even registered to vote until recently—Diaz has emerged as the front-runner among eight candidates vying to become Miami's next mayor. His work as one of the attorneys who argued Elián should stay in America is serving him well. The mayoral election, to be held in two months, is shaping up as an Elián referendum.

It rained hard before the Overtown–Palmetto game. Although the rain has stopped, dark black clouds still hover over downtown's skyscrapers, which are visible from the field. Orange mud bubbles up from the grass, making the field appear to be covered in butterscotch pudding.

"Overtown has a decent defense," says Palmetto assistant coach Santaris Lee. "It's not as good as ours, but it's decent. They've got *no* offense. Campos is a smart-ass coach. He'll expose them."

In the first half, the Rattlers don't need their offense. Thanks to a punt return for a score, Overtown scores the initial touchdown. Jarmaine—Trick Daddy's brother—pulls off his helmet, rips off his shoulder pads and jersey, and unwinds the rows of silver duct tape that hold up his too-small game pants. "Fuck this," he says, quitting on the spot. At halftime, three more Raiders join Jarmaine's mutiny by refusing to return to the field. One sits on his helmet, his face in his hands, his eyes glaring at the mud covering his cleats.

"Let's suck it up," exhorts Coach Lee. "Your dad didn't raise no quitter, dog."

The second half: Four straight sacks of the Palmetto quarterback have the Overtown fans hopping on their bleachers and tapping staccato blasts on air horns. A Palmetto punt travels one pathetic yard. A Palmetto fumble in the end zone late in the game gives Overtown a second score. The Rattlers coach tumbles to the ground in an exaggerated pantomime of ecstasy.

"We bad-ass! We bad-ass!" The chorus from the Overtown bleachers hurts Campos's ears. He slogs through the mud toward the bus with his arms folded across his chest. The thick fingers of one hand reach up to stroke the gray hairs of his beard. His Raiders, undefeated two years in a row, own a record of two wins and two losses—hardly the stuff of champions. A good carpenter is never supposed to blame his tools, but Campos, the self-described best coach in America, isn't about to take the blame for the loss.

"When you get in a tough situation, that's when your players show up," he says. "Unfortunately, that's when your nonplayers show up too. We have a yellow streak. Our guys are quitters."

Chapter 12

Pete

Coach Pete slumps home from his job unloading trucks. Without saying a word, the Warriors defensive coordinator passes his teenage son, who sits in the dark living room watching music videos on BET. In the kitchen Pete opens the refrigerator to grab a sixteen-ounce can of Budweiser. Popping the top, he takes a sip deep enough to necessitate the opening of another can, which he grabs before closing the door. He carries the fresh beer into his bedroom. In one slow motion, not stopping, as if he were a mountain climber focusing only on his next step, he pulls off one steel-toed boot, then the other. He tugs his T-shirt over his head and tosses it on the floor. He pulls off his pants. Clad only in socks and boxers, he reaches for a pack of cigarettes swimming on the bedspread, tapping one out.

Pete lights up. Smoke snakes from his nose to the ceiling. As he sits on the edge of the bed, his shoulders droop, his eyes glaze, the ash on his cigarette lengthens. He starts to lift the cigarette toward his lips. Before his hand reaches his mouth he stops. His expression changes from blank to pain. He forgot about Phillip.

"Shit," he says, dropping the cigarette to his knee. Flecks of ash fall to the floor. "Shit."

Phillip quit the Warriors after the Palmetto loss. No one's seen or heard from his since. Pete promised he would stop by the boy's house tonight to check up on him. Pete rests the cigarette on an ashtray, then gently snubs it out so he can finish it later. He pulls his work pants back on, then his boots. From his dresser he retrieves a yellow Warriors polo. He throws a jacket over his shoulders and steps out to his car.

"We tried with Phillip," he says as he drives east on 54th Street. "I heard certain things about his household but I don't know how true they is or nothing like that."

Pete parks on a street bathed in a darkness cut only by a glow from inside Phillip's house. A deflated plastic football lies on the lawn. Phillip's pet rabbit rattles a cage off to the side of the house. Pete knocks on the front door. A boy's voice asks who's there.

"It's Coach Pete."

Phillip opens the door. He's wearing baggy nylon shorts and nothing else. He stares at Pete as if struck mute. Phillip's aunt steps into the foyer to see who it is.

"I just wanted to stop by and see why he stopped playing football," Pete says. "We ain't seen him around and, like, I just wanted to make sure everything is okay."

At least one of Phillip's six teachers calls home every day to complain about his disruptive behavior. Phillip is picking on other, weaker kids, the aunt reports. Phillip stands there, a small boy in shorts. His skin is smooth. His stomach protrudes as if he aspires to a beer belly. Out of the corner of his eye he watches a television tuned to BET. Trick Daddy spews a message of poverty and pain through a mouthful of gold teeth.

"He's a gangsta, that's what he is," the aunt says, referring to Phillip and not to the musician. "He watches all this rap on TV and whatnot. That's where he gets his ideas. He likes to be the gangsta. Phillip is very smart. I've had him now like about three years. I adopted him. Right now I'm trying to do the best I can with him. I need some help."

"We're here to help," says Coach Pete.

"Maybe he'll be back next year. It all depends on how he acts, all right?"

As the Warriors stretch before a home game against Coral Reef, head coach Brian Johnson reveals that, without Phillip in the lineup, he's looking for creative ways to turn the season around.

"I put on a second T-shirt," he says. "I woke up today and I wanted to change everything, to look different. I wanted a different shirt. I got rid of my hat, my shorts. I didn't shave my hair or my face. Not today."

While the change in dress may be symbolic, Brian also implemented a host of changes to the Warrior game plan. Most significantly, he's gone back on his word to never tinker with the offense.

"I told Beasley to run less pass plays. And the ones they run are all going to be home runs for touchdowns, not for dinky ten-yard gains."

The Warriors win, 24–0.

Brian, emboldened, takes full control. At practice the following week he introduces the Warriors to even more new plays. Diamond, at wide receiver, runs reverses and slant routes absent from the complicated preseason playbook. Not only are the short-yardage plays a rejection of Beasley's vaunted Georgia Southern system, but the plays also seem out of sync with Brian's stated intention of passing only for home runs.

"This *is* a home run," he asserts as he watches Diamond drop an easy lob. "These plays, if they do them right, will be home runs every time. These are plays *I* like, plays I'm trying to get Beasley to put into the offense."

Diamond jogs back to the huddle. Feigning exhaustion, he flops onto his back, his cleats in the air. Brian is not amused.

"Turn over!"

Diamond turns over.

"I want you to run these plays right," Brian barks. "If you don't run these plays, we gonna run laps. You got that? I want perfection! I try to be nice out here. I been nice out here all season long. I'm not gonna be nice no more. Give me twenty-five."

Diamond and his offensive teammates squeeze out push-ups. The defense works with Coach Pete, who's standing apart from the team. His teeth bite down on a steel whistle. A Dolphins baseball cap pulled low shades his eyes. He stands wide on his legs, his arms folded across his chest. When he flexes his right arm, the bicep that rises is missing a large piece, as if someone removed muscle fibers with an ice cream scoop. Or, as it turns out, a knife.

"When I got out of the Army I used to spend a lot of time hanging out," he says after ejecting the whistle and letting it dangle on a nylon cord. "You know, just hanging out where I wasn't supposed to be hanging out. One night this dude came at me with a knife. It was one of those knives on the side, a switchblade. It felt like I'd been punched. He sliced me clear from here to here." Pete runs a finger along a thick scar that winds like a railroad track from his elbow up to his shoulder, then down and across to his right nipple. "Man, that hurt like hell. He just left me there to die, and I thought I *was* gonna die I lost so much blood. Fortunately, I was so hyped that, even with my arm like, hanging off, I got in a car and drove myself to the hospital. It messed me up real bad, though."

Pete looks out at the practice field, where his defenders dance through the drill. "I learned a lesson, I guess: Stop hanging out."

When practice ends, and as Coach Brian huddles up the team, the street agent McAdoo steps forward. He'd been watching practice from a perch near the concrete light post. He unfolds one of his giant homemade posters. "For Our Heroes in Station 12," the sign states. At McAdoo's request, the Warriors autograph the poster, which will hang in the weight room of the fire station behind the game-day football field. When everyone's signed the poster, McAdoo introduces a public speaker.

"Good evening, gentlemen," says a young man in a green polo, jeans, and gleaming white sneakers. A silver cell phone levitates on his belt. His head is shaved and polished as smooth as his speaking voice.

"Good evening, gentlemen," he repeats. "How are you tonight?"

"Good," the Warriors answer in monotonous unison. Stevie, the Deion Sanders protégé, tacks on some civility: "How are you?"

"I'm good too," the speaker says. "Thanks for asking."

The speaker, a friend of McAdoo's, warns the Warriors about the danger of investing all their dreams in a future in pro sports. He tells the team that there are 15,000 athletes playing college sports, yet only 350 players in the NFL.

"Break it down, gentlemen. That's less than three percent," he says. "You need to know how to use football as a tool to get your education. I played basketball down here in Miami. I went on to school for free, basically. I played on the basketball team and that was all well and good, but what happens when you get injured, what happens when someone runs a 4-3 and undercuts your legs? Then what are you going to do? I was able to get an education out of it. I studied mathematics, I got a degree in chemistry. All of you can do it too. Don't let anybody tell you that books are not cool. When you grow up you will find out how cool it is. Do you understand that?"

"Yes, sir."

"Everyone wants to go to UM or FSU. If you don't have your grades, they don't want you. Some of the best athletes ever from around here never played on Sunday. Why? Because they didn't have the grades. When all is said and done, your education is what you need to be a productive member of society. You need to have the right attitude. Any questions, gentlemen?"

"Where you play ball?"

"I played at Fort Valley State."

"You on TV?"

"Yeah, I was on TV. Not that much but I was on TV."

"Why you not play football?"

"Some people's skills are stronger in different areas."

"Why you stop playing basketball?"

"'Cause that's what happened. If you don't get invited to the NBA then you can't play anymore. You have to move on with your life and become a productive member of society. You have to get on with your life."

"Where's Fort Valley State?"

"In Valdosta, Georgia." The speaker glances at McAdoo, who rolls his eyes.

"Look, gentlemen, what I want to tell you is that you got a better chance of winning the lottery than you do of playing in the NFL. What I'm hoping for is when you grow up and make it, you got to come out right back and stand in my place here. Can y'all do that for me?"

"Yes, sir."

"Okay, then, clap it up."

The team clusters for the end-of-practice cheer. Coach Pete wades into the center of the huddle.

"I didn't know we were having a speaker today," Pete says. "I was just telling one of y'all all about education and how important it is. I wouldn't be here telling it to you every day if I didn't personally know how important it is. If you don't get grades, colleges just ain't gonna want to deal with you. Take education seriously, men. Don't be like me. Man, don't be like me. Be better than me."

*   *   *

On Saturday, October 6, the Warriors tie Suniland, 6–6. Although it's the second week in a row without a loss, the coaches and parents are not satisfied. Suniland, like Coral Reef the week before, is a traditionally weak team. Blame for the disappointing tie falls on the offense, which, at least historically, should have scored more points. The referees didn't help any, either.

"I'm telling you, it was a conspiracy, man," Pete says on Sunday afternoon, one hour into a phone call with a former Warriors coach who moved to Atlanta. Pete remains dressed in the full uniform of a Warriors hat, polo shirt, and black shorts. Several trophies from better Warrior seasons glitter in his dining room. A picture of the national championship team hangs in a frame on a wall in the living room.

Two leather couches face a 36-inch television. The Miami Dolphins are playing in Seattle, and a crowd of neighbors has turned out to watch. Periodically a friend strolls in with a six-pack or two. Pete requests the beers be stowed in the freezer so that they will frost by the start of the second half. So many friends have complied that the freezer overflows with cans. The two couches are crammed with bodies cheering on Miami's pro team.

"You got to excuse me," says Pete's wife, Renee, after an interception by Dolphins quarterback Jay Fiedler provokes a flurry of profanity. "I'm going to be drinking, smoking, and swearing over here."

Some twenty kids dart in and out of the house. Stevie and Bobby from the 95s stayed over last night to play video games on Pete's PlayStation 2. Other boys grab drumsticks from the pile of chicken Pete cooked earlier on his backyard grill. The chicken is washed down with fruity sodas and topped off with an unlimited supply of frosted yellow cupcakes Renee purchased this morning at the Winn-Dixie down the street.

Pete's house, which sits just two blocks from Hadley Park, is a de facto community center. Warriors and their friends splash and dive into his backyard pool, one of the only pools in the neighborhood. Any kid who brings in a report card—any kid, from anywhere—receives a dollar from Renee's wallet for every A. The kids are welcome every day, any time of the day 'cept for Friday night, when Renee, Pete, and their grown friends "get their groove on" as she says. The aftermath from Friday's party is still evident on Sunday. The mob watching the Dolphins shares the living room with a platoon of empty Budweiser tallboys, stacked on top of every table, on the television, and even atop an aquarium bubbling next to the TV.

"To me life is good, you know?" says Renee. "We have a lot of faults and problems and stuff like that, but what can you do? What can you do about your problems? Sit here and worry and go and commit suicide? Or laugh? All the joys that life has given you, enjoy it."

Pete hangs up the phone, pulls up a dining room chair, and sits between the two couches. He and Renee inherited their house (and an unsatisfied mortgage) when his mother died. Over the years they've watched many of their friends leave Liberty City for Georgia or the Carolinas. They've stayed behind.

Pete graduated from Northwestern High with absolutely no idea what he wanted to do with his life. The Army seemed as good an option as any, and Pete stayed in the service for eight years. Since his discharge he's worked mostly at warehouses loading and unloading trucks. Just a few months ago he was laid off from a job in nearby Hialeah. Now he works near the stucco subdivisions of Miramar, a half-hour drive north in Broward County.

"I like being at that park, you know, to make sure the boys are coming up right and don't go through what I'm going through," Pete says. "Back when I was coming up I was an independent-type kid, and I didn't have no focus. I would never have thought that football was the ticket out. Nowadays it's publicized so much. Take Pop Warner ball: That's what gets you into high school, which is what gets you into college, which is from where you make the pros. I didn't know that. People say there's too much faith in getting to the pros and all, but even if it is too much faith, I feel that's still a good thing. They know if they do go to college and make it to the NFL they gonna get the big payday."

The TV blares a Dolphin touchdown. Miami leads Seattle 23–0. Renee flicks the ash from her cigarette into an empty Budweiser can. Pete lifts his can, rattles it a few times to determine it's empty, then puts it back down on the floor between his feet.

"The point I was trying to make to the kids at practice the other day was, you know: Don't be like me. 'Cause you see how I come out there at practice sometimes straight from my job with my arms and my head hanging down. With the self-esteem—I wouldn't say smarts—but with the self-esteem that I have and stuff like that, I should have been a better person in life than what I am."

Renee puts her hand on Pete's knee. "You ain't so bad," she says.

"I mean a better person in life as far as I should have gotten my education. I should have got a college education, then I could be in, you know, a better station."

"But who's to say?" Renee counters. "You might have made that money, then you still be out there doing what you doing. But if you did make more money then you probably wouldn't be with me. Then you wouldn't know how to dance and do all that kind of stuff. You wouldn't know how to dance at all. I introduce all that to your life."

"Whatever!" Pete says, breaking into laughter. "That's what I mean when I make statements like, 'Be better than me,' or whatever. You got to get a good job, get an education and set your own path, be that in sports or business or whatever."

He looks at the TV. On the screen, millionaires run around a field of artificial grass.

"I screwed up. I know I screwed up, you know. Bottom line."

"You didn't screw up," Renee says.

"No," Pete insists. "I screwed up."

Chapter 13

The Game

"I was a wide receiver. I was tall, not too athletic, but I could catch," recalls George Knox. "I remember going out for a pass and it was all unfolding. The ball was in the air and I was being covered by this white guy and I was thinking, 'I've got to make him respect me.' That sounds kinda foolish now but that's honestly what I was thinking. It was the first time any of us had ever played against whites and it was the first time the whites had ever played against blacks. Our whole history was in the air with that pass. 'I must catch this ball because if I don't he'll think blacks aren't as good as whites.' The reputation of our race, even the entire history of race relations in America, is up in the air and it's all unfolding in a microsecond. I'm just thinking, 'Lord, don't let me drop this ball.'"

* * *

Street is a free weekly newspaper published by the *Miami Herald*. It's supposedly aimed at younger readers disenfranchised from daily newspapers. The tabloid features club listings, movie reviews, and a few thin articles. *Street* debuted a few years ago and, at its inception, ran brief man-on-the-street profiles of the bartenders, DJs, and models who constitute Miami Beach's club scene. One young black man said his favorite activity was swimming in the ocean, his favorite club was Level or 321 or whatever was the hot club of the moment. Standard stuff. Yet there was more value to his profile than usual. When he was asked to name something unique about Miami he replied: Everyone assumes I'm poor.

The highest-profile blacks in Miami play for the Dolphins. Jason Taylor, Ricky Williams. Rap music provides the luminaries of Luther Campbell and Trick Daddy, along with his female side-kick Trina. After that? U.S. Representative Carrie Meek, City Commissioner Arthur Teele, and a few ministers. From there the roster thins considerably. A Miamian who visits Atlanta is struck by the integrated middle class in that city, the capital of the South. Not so in Miami. Black skin means "everyone assumes I'm poor."

George Knox was born in Jacksonville in 1943. After graduating from Michigan State, he enrolled in law school at the University of Miami. He's been here pretty much ever since. Knox served the City of Miami as its first-ever black city attorney. He's a member of the Orange Bowl Committee, an indicator of his station in the establishment. A business magazine named Knox one of the 100 most powerful people in town. For that title alone he may be Miami's most successful black man.

For the past twenty years Knox has focused his law practice on public policy land use, and on lobbying for clients before county and city governments. His ninth-floor office affords him a view of the summertime swarm of Brazilian tourists streaming in and out of downtown's many electronics stores. On one of his office walls hangs a poster of Albert Einstein, an honorary degree from historically black Florida Memorial College (where he serves on the board), and a proclamation declaring it George Knox Day in the City of Miami.

Until he left Jacksonville for college at age sixteen, Knox lived in a segregated housing project that bordered a white neighborhood. It was while living in this project that he came to play in what his friends have come to call The Game.

✦ ✦ ✦

"I lived in the shadow of the newly constructed Interstate 95, in what was affectionately called West Springfield. I lived two doors from the liquor store that probably proved to be my father's demise.

"Springfield was identified as one of the earliest communities in Jacksonville, dating back to the Civil War. The line of demarcation—the demilitarized zone, if you will—between black West Springfield and white East Springfield was this place called Springfield Park, which was a white park that featured a Confederate soldier with his back facing the North. It had a swimming pool and that sort of thing. Blacks would walk along the street adjacent to that park and we could only look over at what was going on.

"Through the time I graduated from high school, blacks had no access to any public facilities such as parks. We drank from colored drinking fountains and we were not allowed in the movie theaters. We were allowed to shop in the department stores, but there was never any dialogue, nor was there any social contact, at that time between the races. It was the perpetuation of the image that blacks were consumers and had access to commercial facilities in order to purchase goods, but that was the extent of the relationship.

"Football was the most popular sport when I was growing up. When it came to following football, blacks in the community knew everything there was to know about the white high schools: who the players were, who the star was, who the mascot was, what the team colors were. We'd read the newspaper and we'd know what [all-white] Landon High School and Jackson High School were doing. On the other side of the *Florida Times-Union* newspaper was all the news "for and about colored people." We knew the white population wasn't reading about the activities at my high school or at any black high schools.

"For instance, there was this black star at the black high school who on one night had scored six touchdowns. Now, on the same night, the sort-of all-American at the white high school gained a pedestrian sixty-one yards in his game. Yet the headline in the newspaper was related to the white player who gained sixty-one yards. And the general public didn't even know that the black player had scored six touchdowns on the same night. There was this yearning for blacks to demonstrate their skills to the larger population—first to gain respect for their skills, and also to have some recognition of the very existence of the black community.

"It went beyond just football. But because football is the sport of choice and because football has always been such a part of the culture of many, many communities, football—especially high school football—was sort of the focal point.

"There were very specific neighborhoods in Jacksonville where I grew up that had their own football team consisting of the boys that didn't make the team at the high school. When Durkeeville was playing Blodgett Homes on Sunday afternoon—those were two prominent projects in Jacksonville—it became a pretty big deal. I played on a team. We were just scruffy little part-time athletes who got together on weekends, but our games kept getting more and more elaborate. We would scavenge football shoes and we would get discarded footballs and we had to find ways to provide our own equipment and transportation, but still, it got to be a pretty exciting thing.

"Almost on impulse we gravitated toward Springfield Park, where we knew whites our same age played football on Sunday afternoons. We'd be out playing football and they'd be out playing football too. So we started occasionally throwing our football over there, to their side. They'd throw it back. We eventually got to the point where all of the white players were on one side behind the curb and we were on the other side behind the curb. Almost by sign language we started to suggest that we might want to get together and play a game.

"The suggestion was received well by both sides. There's a natural curiosity. Anybody that you've been isolated from and anybody you perceive to be different, you want to find out how you measure up against. They were just as curious as we were about how they would fare against blacks.

"It was a matter of the most sophisticated diplomacy in order to set this up. We discussed the logistics of the game: how many people on the team, whether it was going to be touch below the belt or touch above the belt or whether we were going to play tackle football without helmets or shoulder pads. Eventually we settled on the ground rules. We set a date that was far enough off into the future that everybody could sort of get prepared and sort of spread the word.

"I probably didn't sleep for weeks in anticipation of The Game, as we called it. I washed and rewashed whatever it was I decided I was going to wear. We called our uniforms "mammy-made," which means that you didn't buy them, you sort of pinned them together with whatever your mother could provide to you. We would paint numbers on white T-shirts with liquid black shoe polish we hoped wouldn't run. I made an absolute point of being certain I didn't have to play a football game in tennis shoes. Discarded high-top football cleats were the only cleats we could find. The color had faded out of the leather so we dyed our shoes so they would shine and be black—honestly. We went out and bought new fresh white strings and it took us all night long to lace them up. I made sure I had tape on my ankles and tape on my wrists and I did everything I possibly could to emulate some superstar in the National Football League.

"Each of my teammates did the same thing. It was like we put on our game faces. It was like we didn't want to talk too much about it because we didn't want to break out of our zone of concentration. It was utterly the most important thing we had envisioned doing. It was right up there with taking the SAT test or any other major activity in our lives. It was everything to us.

"There had been a tacit agreement that this had to take place in secret. I believe that on both sides, on both teams, there was a reluctance to let our parents know about the game, because we believed that our parents would discourage it or even prohibit it from happening. Everybody whispered about the game to their girlfriends, because this was a real big deal.

"We all met in Springfield Park on a Sunday afternoon. The pregame was as formal as any official football game. There were volunteer referees from both sides that both parties agreed to and there was the flip of the coin and there was the mutual shaking of hands. The white kids didn't wear uniforms. Once again, it's the relativity of importance that was attached to the game."

🏈 🏈 🏈

"I'd say halfway through the entire experience is when I caught the pass. Prior to that time it was a stalemate, zero–zero. Nobody was getting anyplace, in part because all of us were nervous and trying to be good sports and that sort of thing and in part because we were feeling each other out. My play became important to the game because it was the breakout.

"I can remember everything that occurred on this particular play almost in super-slow motion. I was the wide receiver. I got behind the defender. The quarterback saw me and he launched the ball. It was a long pass, and as the ball was coming down I was filled with anxiety. One: I knew I couldn't drop it because I knew this was my only chance in life to outdo a white peer. Number two: I felt that the whole world, every aspect of black America, was riding on my ability to catch this pass. All of these things were going into my mind as the ball was descending into my hands. And I was terrified at the prospect of dropping the ball.

"So much of the significance of that pass goes beyond what's ordinary in sports. It meant *a lot* that I caught the ball. You gain somebody's respect when you beat them. It became critically important. The most important thing I have ever done and would ever think about doing was simply to catch this ball. And at that moment it was falling into my hands.

"I scored a touchdown on the play, and when I did, the guy I beat was on the ground. After I crossed the goal line and even after my friends and I celebrated, I looked down at him and he looked up at me. And he did nothing more than nod. That nod meant 'Good play.' That nod meant 'You beat me fair and square' and a lot of other things. It was a definite show of respect.

"And the fact is we scored first. That raised the stakes for everybody, especially them. We didn't believe the white kids wanted to go home and say they just got beat by a bunch of blacks in a football game. The hitting got harder and people got much more serious. And that's what I mean: The respect that we gained is that they rose to the occasion, so to speak. That's where this tough running back came from. We couldn't do anything to stop this guy, because he was obsessed—obsessed with his own success, the success of his team, and with not having to go home and face somebody about losing. That fullback managed to run for a touchdown.

"As soon as he scored, tension got released. I wish I could really vividly describe it, but we were somewhat relieved they had scored. It was the ultimate display of sportsmanship, that this demonstration project should not result in one team or the other winning. It's a real weird feeling. We were relieved that they scored, because we thought we would have had to stay there all day if they hadn't. The winning and losing tension was mitigated a little bit because each of us by that time had proved our point.

"So then we entered into the next phase. Now having proved our point, now having established a mutual measure of respect, let's see who scores again. The tension was that much more heightened, but now we were in kind of a groove. As the tension grew and the game progressed, everybody started to take it far, far more seriously. Everybody started to focus. Amazingly, it wasn't any kind of antagonism. It was sport in its truest sense.

"And that's when the cops came. The cops came and simply directed us to break up the game. They didn't give us any explanation. We felt because of the authority that the cops represented that it was in our best interests that we simply pack up and leave. We couldn't argue with them; we couldn't try to persuade them. And the fellows on the other side didn't want to be in the position of creating a confrontation that was going to call their parents out. So it just essentially dissolved."

🏈 🏈 🏈

"All these years later the memory of that game still lingers. It was the first interaction I'd ever had with a white peer, under any circumstances at all. Maybe it was only important to me and some of my teammates. I dare say it wasn't important to any of the white kids that were involved in the game. But it literally was a life-changing experience for me. It's not far-fetched for me to say my subsequent career was enhanced by that football game. I won't say 'directly,' but it was enhanced by the relationships I was comfortable developing following that game. And following that nod from this guy I had just vanquished.

"From my experience, that's kind of the feeling that still exists to this day in high school and Pop Warner football leagues. People in Liberty City take it far, far more seriously than their counterparts in Pinecrest. The same social dynamics of dressing up and being on your best behavior are the same when a team from Liberty City drives down to Suniland to play an all-white team. I believe the fundamental dynamics are the same.

"I think it's very important to note that blacks take this far more seriously than whites do. It's easier for whites to become 'color-blind' than it is for blacks not to be color-conscious. I'm aware that I'm black before I go before the county commission or I go into a courtroom. I'm sometimes aware that there's a white lawyer on the other side. And I sometimes feel the same cultural imperative to win because I represent my whole race in a routine argument in a courtroom. It becomes more and more suppressed but it is always present, and in many respects I have not tried to eliminate that feeling, because it is a source of inspiration for me, it makes me work that much harder.

"In many respects, athletic competition—if the competition is arranged along ethnic or racial lines—still represents the only direct opportunity that blacks have to demonstrate excellence, and more importantly, superiority to their white counterparts. That means an awful lot."

Chapter 14

Homecoming

Early October brings a streak of blustery days, some strong enough to elicit a wind advisory. Although the air remains warm enough for shorts, the gusty reminder that the seasons are about to change provides the first excuse to break out the fall wardrobe. Whenever the temperature drops a few degrees, Miami becomes suddenly better dressed. Lincoln Road on Miami Beach adopts a black-leather-coat dress code. Warriors assistant coach Ed gets into the spirit of things, in a long denim coat that matches his baggy blue jeans.

"All right, gentlemen, let's see some Warrior pride out here today," he commands, walking onto the practice field.

When a season is lost, individual games carry greater meaning. The University of Michigan might stumble through a season without a win, but if, on the last game of the year, the Wolverines defeat Ohio State, the season is fundamentally a success. For the 95-pound Warriors, the big one is the homecoming game. A win against Richmond will not only salvage whatever Warrior Pride remains, it could even salvage a miserable season. Warriors win in the final two games, against Richmond and then on the road against the Northwest Falcons, should be enough for the team to squeak into the playoffs with a wild card.

"Now, men, it's homecoming week," Coach Ed says. "We've not lost a homecoming game in I don't know how long. I don't care what our record is we gonna beat Richmond in our house in front of our king and queen. You understand?"

"Yes sir."

As they have all season, the Warriors break off into groups by position. Beasley and Brian work with the offense. Normally that group includes Diamond, but today he is lined up on defense.

"Why? We short!" explains Coach Chico, Pete's assistant. "That how it is sometimes."

Another assistant chimes in: "The thing is, he's playin'. He may have a spirit."

"Diamond showing tremendous heart," adds Chico. "He's scrappy. He's tough. He playin'."

Diamond enjoys his new position. He pursues quarterbacks and running backs with an anger he's never before displayed. When wide receiver Chase runs a pattern that brings him and the ball into Diamond's vicinity, Diamond rams his forearms into Chase's padded chest. Foom! The wide receiver's torso snaps violently. He falls onto his back. Though Chase is not seriously hurt, Diamond, standing over Chase's prone body, stares him down as if he wishes he'd killed him.

"I get to hit somebody," Diamond says after jogging to the sideline for a breather. "I get to hit the person, then I get to mash 'im, then I get to slam 'im and make 'im run to their daddy for advice. When you hit somebody, they get afraid of you."

On Saturday, two inflatable fun houses bounce on the patchy grass where the 95s normally practice. In one house, young boys scale a climbing wall, slide down a long chute, and climb back up again. In the other house, shoeless kids leap as if traversing the weightless surface of the moon. A man sets up a mixing board in front of a bank of stereo speakers.

"Check one. Check one. Checking."

In addition to the fun house floats and the live DJ and the booths selling conch, chicken, and sodas, the Warriors' homecoming features more than a little pageantry. At halftime of the 95-pound game, two florists race out to midfield to erect a gazebo archway. Volunteers cart in six Ionic columns molded in white plastic and topped off with bouquets of yellow roses. Cheerleaders tether strings of helium-inflated black, yellow, and white balloons that stretch up toward the cloud cover. The DJ sparks up a recording of "Pomp and Circumstance."

The coaches of each weight division have nominated a homecoming king, to be paired with a queen selected for each weight from the cheerleading squads. The winners were originally to be determined via an essay contest about the destruction of the World Trade Center, but that theme was scrapped for lack of interest. Now the winners are the boys and girls who've sold the most raffle tickets. Grand prize: a 13-inch television.

The boys wear tuxedos. The girls wear white dresses suitable, at least on the younger queens, for a first communion or confirmation. Tiaras levitate in hair straightened into taffy pyramids seven inches tall. The youngest homecoming king is a boy nicknamed Tit Tat. The five-year-old, who has never before worn a suit, marches to midfield with exaggerated rigidity. The 95-pound king, wide receiver Sherdale Stephens, joins Tit Tat, six other kings, and all eight queens in a line at midfield. The DJ reads a prepared statement:

"The overall king and queen of Liberty City Optimists are Mr. Michael Lewis and beautiful Kandra Collins."

A teenager in a white suit with a black dress shirt steps forward to the applause of a thousand people. His queen accepts her crown from last year's queen. The new royal couple hold scepters aloft. Moms and aunts snap shutters on one of the two or three disposable cameras each of them is carrying.

Sherdale marches back to join his team in the south end zone. (He was the only king allowed to stay in his football uniform during the ceremony.) The score at halftime is 0–0, and Richmond has outplayed the Warriors from the opening kickoff. The only reason the Giants aren't wining is because, late in the second quarter, their wide receiver dropped an easy touchdown pass.

"They not showed up," Coach Ed huffs, referring to the Warriors. "Richmond plays chippy. They oldest coach only something like nineteen years old. We should be killin' 'em." Ed slaps Sherdale on the helmet the king has just pulled back on. "Play your best football out there!"

Richmond starts the second half in possession of the ball. The defense holds pretty well, to a point—every time possession is about to change, the Warriors make a mistake that gives Richmond new life. On a key fourth-down stop, Liberty City is penalized fifteen yards for "spearing," or using a helmet like a battering ram. On another fourth down, Brian and Pete shout at the players to watch the ball so they don't step offside. The Warriors step offside anyway. Another Richmond first down. Soon thereafter a touchdown and an extra point. Seven–zip.

"Shit," mutters Coach Pete. "That's pretty much it."

Brian tosses his clipboard to the ground. "Sheeeeeiiiiiit," he hisses. Beasley, the offensive coordinator, can say nothing. His hands cross behind his neck, his eyes shut, his mouth hangs open as if awaiting instructions. A linebacker slumps to the bench, his face mask propped in his hands.

"This is the gridiron, man," shouts the boy's stepfather, his arms draped over the chain-link fence that surrounds the field. "This ain't no swimming pool. You have plenty of pain out there. You need to wipe your face and go out there and play like a man. All you got to do is you suck it up! You a defensive lineman. That's where the game is played, in pain. Quit playing soft! You playing like a girl. You worry about your bumps and bruises when the game is over and you soaking in your tub."

* * *

Redemption is possible. There is a Hollywood movie scenario that could unfold. Richmond could choke away its four downs. The Warriors could regain possession. With a fresh set of downs of its own, Liberty City would have four chances to throw a "home run" pass for the game-tying touchdown. The Warriors would still have life. Playoffs and everything. Other teams in the league aren't playing so hot either. Orlando—as impossible a dream as that had been just a week ago—is not out of the question.

And that's exactly how the script unfolds. At least for a while. Richmond fails to gain a yard on three straight running plays. Needing ten yards for a first down to ice the game, the Richmond quarterback throws up a wobbly, wildly inaccurate pass that drifts well out of bounds before falling to the ground incomplete. Warrior ball.

But wait. In his glee at the change of possession, Stevie, the cornerback who idolizes "Prime Time" Deion Sanders, runs over and picks up the ball. He holds it aloft. Because he is a showman like Sanders, and because the incomplete pass means the defense has infused Liberty City with fresh life, Stevie spikes the ball on the ground.

"Tweeeeet!" Whistles blow. Yellow flags fly. Unsportsmanlike conduct. Fifteen-yard penalty. Richmond retains possession. Stevie is immediately pulled from the game, which now really is all but over. Brian grabs him by the face mask.

"I thought we'd got the ball," Stevie argues.

"Shut up!" Brian shouts, glaring at Stevie, his eyes aflame behind his blue sunglasses. He sees in Stevie's unapologetic face the shards of the national championship dream. All that talk about being a man, about proving he can coach at this level. All those nights and weekends in his room, on his computer, drafting an offense. All those practices. All the bullshit from the parents. As Brian strengthens his grip on the face mask, Stevie unloads more excuses. In his loudest tone, with enough wind to blow Stevie down if he wasn't holding on to the boy's face mask, Brian liberates his disappointment at the bitter end of a long, frustrating season.

"Shut UP!"

The referee's whistle confirms another Warrior defeat. Brian lets go of the face mask. Stevie runs off. The Richmond players collapse in unison at midfield. "You all know what time it is?" one of them shouts. "It's our time!" The bank of speakers sparks to life. Too appropriately, the DJ spins "Ugly," a rap anthem by Bubba Sparxxx.

● ● ●

"It's very, very frustrating to me to put your heart into something and see it go a way you don't like. You got to look at yourself and say, 'Man, what the fuck am I doin' wrong.'"

Brian sits on the rear bumper of his van, which he's parked on the practice field. Players pull off their helmets and throw them on the ground in disgust, denting the turf. Tears fall freely. Coach Chico sits on the bumper next to Brian. Coach Pete stands just to the side, sipping from a green bottle of Heineken camouflaged by a brown paper bag. A father walks over to drape an arm around Brian's shoulder. "Tough season," he says.

"'Tough' ain't the word," Brian replies.

"If I could climb to the top of that goalpost and jump off and end it now I would," Chico offers.

Brian takes a swig of Budweiser from a longneck bottle he's hidden behind the bumper.

"It was one hell of an experience, huh?" he says. "They taught me a lot more than I taught their asses. One big learnin' experience. Next year there's going to be none of this democracy shit. I'll be running the same kind of offense, only we gonna start it from the beginning of the year and I'm gonna be calling the plays, too. Ain't nobody else but me."

When there's nothing more to look forward to in one season, the only thing to anticipate is the season to come. Pete and Chico toss around the roster of next year's expected returnees. Terrance and Ruben are both only eight years old, so they'll be back. Andre will be back at wide receiver, and he's good. Sippio should return too. So will Diamond.

"Do I want Diamond back?" Brian asks Chico.

"Yeah," Chico says. "Diamond all right."

The grass in front of the van reeks of sweaty jerseys and shoulder pads. Some of the boys have run off in pursuit of snow cones and barbecue chicken wings. A few boys remain on the grass, awash in the pain of a sorry season. One boy is crying harder than anyone else. He lies in a fetal position, his knees pulled to his smooth face. It takes a minute to recognize that the boy is Stevie.

"You better check yourself, man," says Stevie's grandmother, a large woman with curlers in her hair. She stands over his inert body, gazing down as if she were a giant. "You better check yourself. I don't know what your problem is."

Stevie climbs up to his feet and buries himself in this grandmother's substantial bosom. "We lost," he warbles, sucking in massive gulps of humid air. "It was our homecoming and we lost. We gonna be one of the worst damn teams in the league!"

"All right," she says, wiping his tears. "All right." She bends down to untie his cleats. From a canvas bag she pulls out a pair of Air Jordan basketball sneakers for him to wear home.

Coach Ed picks this moment to approach the van. He surveys the landscape of crying kids, more with disgust than empathy. "You all beat yourselves," he spits.

"Don't be saying that when they already down," snaps Stevie's grandmother. "You should be making 'em feel better."

"The season's over," Ed says, scanning for the supply of Budweisers. "You all beat yourselves."

The beers are in the van, in a cooler next to a box of team photos. Stevie, after he gathers himself, walks over to Brian to collect his pictures. Brian flips until he finds a close-up shot of Stevie, who is the only player with a gold medallion dangling over the collar of his uniform.

"This is what happens when you play sports," Brian tells the boy. "This is what you put yourself into. Whatever comes out, keep your head up. Don't ever cry. Ain't nothing wrong with being angry."

He hands Stevie his photos.

"See you Tuesday," Brian says. "Right, Stevie?"

Stevie nods agreement. Practice on Tuesday, just like always. One more game next Saturday. Stevie walks off with his head bowed. Once he is ten feet from the van, he buries his face back in his grandmother's chest.

Chapter 15

Last Practice

In late October, on an overcast Wednesday, a soft wind rustles the palm trees shading Hadley Park's Olympic pool. The last game of the 95-pound season is on Saturday, on the road at the Northwest Boys & Girls Club. According to the latest standings, there remains a slim, almost purely mathematical chance that the Warriors can still make the playoffs. Everything will have to fall the team's way, the biggest obstacle being the need to actually win, and against a good team no less. That's something no one really believes is possible anymore. The mood in the park matches the gray clouds swirling overhead. There is disappointment. There is even anger.

Brian's got to go. That's pretty much it. His days as a head coach are numbered with a single digit. A losing season? In a park with all this talent? Un-uh. Nope. Not acceptable. It's one thing to lose a game in the playoffs. That's not good, but that happens. But to lose almost every game all year long? That just *doesn't* happen. Brian's already cost the 95-pounders and their parents a whole season of their lives. There's no way he should have a chance to mess up next year too. Change, like the coming relief of autumn, is in the air.

For weeks now parents have been siding up to Sam Johnson, the Warrior's founder and main administrator. Some work subtly, suggesting in the middle of a conversation that Brian might not have the stuff. Other parents are more overt: Brian's a phony. Get him out of there.

"Brian, I feel for him," says Sam, parked at the picnic bench outside the trailer that serves as his office. It's the same bench from the registration-day picnic back in July. A heart carved into the wood tabletop holds a splash of rainwater. "The rumors that be going around about him, they in *my* face, but they ain't coming in *his* face with it."

Sam comes out to the picnic bench when he wants to be left alone. In the trailer, where he usually works, the phone never stops ringing. Someone is always asking him to sign something, or to look at something, or to solve some problem. He's ducked outside with his typical light reading, in this case a seventy-five-page draft of the fiscal year 2002 action plan. He's turned off his cell phone. In front of him a Styrofoam container overflows with conch and shrimp, breaded and fried. Sam has already doused his food with mustard, hot sauce, salt, and tartar sauce. He picks up a clear packet of mayonnaise, contemplates it for a second, then puts it down.

"After being put in the hospital I hadn't had my seafood like I want, so I got me some conch," he says. "But I've had no caffeine in six months. No red meat. No pork. If the doctor tells me that's out, then don't worry about it, that's out."

A thick wad of cotton protrudes from Sam's neck, held in place by a large swatch of clear tape. The cotton covers a catheter where his doctor can insert an IV. The catheter is a blessing, says Sam, who has endured IVs inserted into a vein near his groin. He waves his plastic fork in the direction of his shoulder.

"I had a little knot under there and ignored it," he explains. "This shirt was sticking out like I had a tit. I can't be neglecting myself. I thought I was unselfish and committed and idealistic and I almost put myself in the ground."

He picks up another forkful of conch, looks at the pastiche of sauces he's applied to it, then drops the fork back down. "If I were to die, then this thing would go straight into chaos. This thing, the Warriors and the Optimist Club, isn't about the budget or the system. It's the human element."

Sam is the human element. After eleven years of football and baseball and cheerleading and basketball, he remembers the names and family histories of almost every boy and girl who has spent even one season in the program. He's filled out every grant application for a new scoreboard or a new irrigation system or new youth-sized footballs, and has overseen the money those grants have generated. He lobbies the city and county commissioners for additional funding. He still lives in Liberty City, just so he can track the temperature of the community. He knows, for instance, that this is a county weekend, meaning "everyone who gets a check from the government will be drinking and having themselves a ball. There'll be a lot of foolishness around. Gunshots and the like. The kids see all this stuff." He sees all this stuff too.

Sam is the one who battles with parents who argue that the $120 registration fees for football are too high. Before he gives out a scholarship, he goes over parents' budgets with them. If parents smoke, he'll ask them to stop and put the money toward football. If they drink a twelve-pack a day, he'll ask them to cut back. No one has to go cold turkey on the liquor—as a former bus driver he's been there, working those kinds of jobs—but he asks them to keep their kids in mind.

"We got more control over spending than we know," he tells them. "When your priorities are to make sure you get your nails done at a cost of a hundred twenty dollars then your boy is taken care of; I don't feel sorry for you. But a grandma on a fixed income who's got to raise her children's children? She don't have to sell me on nothing. You ain't supposed to be doing this, Grandma. She gets a break."

Money is a big issue with Sam. It's something he hears about every day. Parents complain that they can enroll their kids at Gwen Cherry Park for a lot less money, and that the boys over there wear better uniforms besides. The county commission, a government eight times larger than the City of Miami and the source of most of Sam's funding, is rumbling about reducing his grant next year. It's not that the commissioners doubt the value of his program, it's just that there are a lot of other programs out there seeking money too.

The first-ever football Warriors, from eleven season ago, are just starting their senior years in college. Sam knows that a few of those players—especially Antonio Bryant at the University of Pittsburgh—enjoy good odds of turning pro. If they do, and if they give back a slice of their contracts to the park where they started in the game, the Warriors won't have to charge as much in registration fees. The club can grow to reach even more people. The Warriors will be solvent for years. "Completing the cycle," Sam calls it.

"I've got to keep it focused on the right way," he says. "We get people all the time, parents who come up and yell at the coaches, saying, 'You sold them to come play for you saying we'll win a championship and all that.' That's not it. That's not what we're about. They bring their babies here and we don't tell them we'll win a championship or nothing at all. We ain't trying to steal nobody's kids. We've won Super Bowls here, national championships, even though that's not what we're about. I got to give everybody that's a part of the success all the ups and down. Brian's not going anywhere. He strive to win, but win or lose he will always show sportsmanship or whatnot. You strive to win. You strive to learn. If you don't win it don't mean you're not successful. If you strive to win you're a winner."

In the parking lot, a man blasts music on his car stereo. A security guard reads a newspaper. On the grass field the 95s and the other weights are gathering for practice. Sam looks down at his food, which has congealed into a fatty, saucy block. He folds up the Styrofoam lid, hiding the mess from view. He picks up the draft of the budget, gathering everything in a pile under the food.

"Anyway," he says as he heads back for the trailer, "as for Brian, he ain't going anywhere."

* * *

Hurricane season coincides with football season. From the end of July through the end of November, a regular pattern emerges in the weather. Mornings are bright and sunny and hot. By noon, usually, a cloud cover moves in. On a textbook day the rain falls between four and five o'clock. It will fall in blasts heavy enough to overwhelm the sewer system. The working-class suburb of Sweetwater transforms into a Venice of flooded mobile homes. By six o'clock the rain usually stops. By seven o'clock the instant lakes evaporate, leaving few signs the storm ever happened.

Today has followed the typical pattern, at least so far. Morning opened bright, clear, and scorching. By midday wispy pink clouds formed, thickening steadily into late afternoon's gray battleships. Yet at six o'clock, as practice begins at Hadley Park, the rain has not yet fallen. Coach Chico looks skyward and shudders. He can feel it on his skin—a drop in pressure, a deadness that proceeds a certain storm.

"This is the last Wednesday practice of the year," he shouts to Warriors stretching in sloppy lines. "Tighten up! Get hyped!"

Coach Beasley walks the offense through the plan for Saturday's game against the Northwest Boys & Girls Club. The Falcons are traditionally the last game of the year for the Warriors, a sign of the rivalry between the two inner-city powers. Even after all the losses, even after the homecoming embarrassment, a win against Northwest will recoup some face, if not the season. To secure that salvation, Beasley's further trimmed the number of play variations the team will attempt, at Brian's request. The first play of practice, a straightforward handoff to a small running back named Bobby, works perfectly.

"It's looking real good," says Coach Ed as he watches the offensive line. "I'm smiling now. If we looked this good earlier in the season we could have beat half those teams." Coach Pete agrees that Warriors football is spiraling upward. "Next year, we be real good," he says. "Next year this team have it all together and we be good. This year was a test or something."

Over by the concrete light post that marks the 95s' space, the regular crowd of parents and grandparents wait out the practice. Most of the spectators are women—mothers, usually, though a few men pull up lawn chairs to watch a son or nephew scrimmage. In greeting one another, the men invariably employ the same salutation: "coach."

"That's a thing that we do in the culture," explains the uncle of one player. "Whenever a man out here sees another man, and they don't know each other, they call each other 'coach.' It's a sign of respect for what they are doing out here, even if they aren't actually coaching."

Watching a practice in which all the Warriors' age groups share the same big field is like watching a three-dimensional growth chart. The four-year-olds in full pads are so diminutive they look like helmets with cleats. The seven-year-old 85s are taller (if that's the right word) and appear more stable; their heads fit better into their helmets. The 110s are lanky, with long shins and athletic gaits. On a patch of grass over by the tennis courts, the 145s, growing into their adult bodies, look as menacing as professional players.

On sunny days the spectators watching the 95s line up in the shady strip provided by the light pole, moving their lawn chairs every few minutes as the shadow crawls across the field. A woman named Lisa walks over with her daughter.

"I've raised my entire family out here," she says. "I haven't missed a practice or game in years. My daughters are now cheerleaders and my sons are football players at Northwestern High. You know how they said it takes a village to raise a child? That's the dynamic out here."

The Miracle Man—the grandpa of offensive lineman Arlis and his twin brother, Aaron—is a practice regular. He fills paper cups with orange Gatorade, a tonic he provides at every practice, at his own expense. "Except they don't get none when they don't show me some discipline," he says, pouring. Lisa asks him where he got his nickname.

"I was, like, dead!" he replies as he fills more cups. "I was a real heavy smoker, three packs a day. My chest is now all spongy-like. I still get pains in the chest. I've got a pacemaker because it keeps my heart ticking sometimes when it stops. Every time I go back to the hospital they call me the Miracle Man."

When the last cup is full, the Miracle Man looks up in time to nod hello to the Peanut Man, a septuagenarian with an equally terrific moniker. The Peanut Man sells plastic sandwich bags of boiled goobers to the parents in the lawn chairs. "Peanuts!" he cries in a soft, high-pitched whisper. "Peanuts! Peanuts! One dollar!" He makes his rounds most every afternoon. Hundreds of brown shells jut from the dust near the light post as if they were cigarette butts in an ashtray.

A linebacker named Vernon sits out practice near the light pole. He's dressed in black shorts and a yellow T-shirt. His cleats are laced, and his helmet is snapped on, but he's wearing no other pads. He grabs a cup of Gatorade and spills a mouthful through his face mask.

"How come you not practicing?" asks the Miracle Man.

"I hurt my knee," Vernon answers.

"How?"

"I was running and I stop and I start again and I call my brother 'Garbage' and then I tripped over a rock in Antwane's yard and I twisted my knee," he says. "That just goes to show, don't be calling no man 'Garbage.'"

A chocolate aroma tickles Vernon's nose. He turns to see a mother setting down a pan of warm brownies on the card table next to the Gatorade cups. Tit Tat, the five-year-old homecoming king, gets his hand slapped when he tries to peel off the tinfoil shielding the brownies from the threatening rain.

Sounds float in from the other weights. From the five-year-olds groaning through leg lifts on the baseball outfield: "Ain't gonna make it if you ain't got no muscle in your stomach." From the 110s practicing over near the game-day field: "You call that a fucking block? That ain't no block! You don't know what the fuck you even doing!"

A coach from Northwestern High watches the 75-pounders practice. It's never too early to scout potential Bulls. It's also never too early to foster allegiance to his school.

"We go out and drive to each Pop Warner park and see each commissioner," says the coach. He's wearing blue sweatpants and a blue T-shirt embellished with the yellow "Bulls Football" logo.

When a Warrior makes a particularly solid catch or tackle, the coach scribbles in a wire notebook. "This is a park that feeds us a lot of what we have coming up in the development stage."

A running back sweeping toward the sideline trips up on his shoelaces. "Get up, man," the high school coach barks. "Stop feeling sorry for yourself. 'Nother day, 'nother play!"

The temperature plunges ten degrees. Cheerleaders practicing near the parking lot halt construction of a human pyramid to pull on sweatshirts. Beasley orders Antwane to hand off to Bobby. At the snap, Diamond, playing defense, breaks through the offensive line to tackle Antwane before he can even hand off the ball. Diamond jumps up and looks over to Coach Pete, the defensive coordinator.

"How was that?" Diamond asks with a smile. Diamond's mother doesn't come to practices anymore. His uncle Durell doesn't show up either. Diamond makes another tackle. Then another. Then a third.

"Last practice, on Thursday, he tell me, 'Watch me! Watch me,'" says Coach Pete, speaking of Diamond. "He has nobody to watch him play. It means something for me to watch him, just watch him. He needs that."

It starts to rain. Drops at first, then, soon enough, a torrent. Straight sheets of warm water strafe the park. Parents fold up their lawn chairs and scurry for the protection of their cars. The 75s and the 85s break practice and scatter off the field. Head coach Brian Johnson, noting the exodus, decides to join it. He blows his whistle to call the 95s in for a last huddle.

Rain rinses clumps of mud off the helmets encircling him. Brian lifts a hand to get everyone's attention. He opens his mouth to say that practice is called, and that they should come back tomorrow for the last time this season. The words, though, do not come out. Brian gazes down at his players: Antwane, Stevie, Sippio, Diamond, Red, Ruben. With the significant exception of Phillip, everyone is still here. Even after a losing season, a record of six losses, one win, and one tie (plus that one win by forfeit). No playoffs. No Disney

World. Few achievements at all, and, on game days at least, very little fun. Yet everyone is still here.

A moment passes, then another. When Brian looks skyward, rain pelts his eyeglasses. When he looks down at his team he finds his players expectant, waiting for his words. His lips curve into a smile.

"Who wants to stay and practice?" he asks. "You done? Anyone feel like going on? Okay? Okay? Then let's practice!"

A cheer rises above the raindrops. After a few tackles in the mud Diamond's practice jersey melts from white to milk chocolate. Water sprays in Antwane's mouth every time he yells, "Hike!" Stevie choreographs Deion Sanders dance steps just to splash in a widening puddle. Warrior director Sam Johnson, standing under an umbrella near the light post, takes in the scene.

"Other parks think it's all about winning," Sam says. "Out here it has nothing to do with winning. I won't ever get rid of Brian unless he tell me he want to go, and then I'd take him into another room and we'd have a real long talk."

*   *   *

TO: PARENTS OF 95 LB PLAYERS
FROM: 95 LB COACHING STAFF
SUBJ: END OF SEASON

This is the end of a very trying and difficult season for the staff as well as the kids. We set many goals at the beginning of the season for the team in on-field performance and record. Unfortunately, we fell short of that mark.

However, we as a staff want to thank you for all of your support through this year. We feel that even though the season's record does not reflect it, we made an impact on the players for this season. We tried to keep the focus on being better young people in life and not just about football. We saw a lot of promising things from a lot of different kids as the season went on. But if it were not for you, and your timeless support, we would have fell short of even that.

So as we wind down to the end of this era, remind your children that this is only a blink of an eye in a very long life. Also remind them that they have our support in any endeavor they wish to embark on in the future. Though they are your sons, we have a special bond with your kid not just as coach, but also as a friend. And we hope that as they go on in life, we can become not just a memory of this season, but also their biggest fans of seasons to come.

If there is anything that we can do to help you in the future feel free to give us a call. We are still a family in our eyes. Because of that feeling, we don't want any of the kids to be lost by the wayside in their futures. So to you parents, we always stand here waiting in the wings, vigilant as ever as your child moves through the program. And for those kids who have the ability to return, and try 95 lb. football one more time, we will be ready for next year. And more than anything, we will welcome you back with a renewed vigor and determination.

> FOR ALL WHO WALK THIS PATH,
> FOR ALL WHO SEE WITH SEEING EYES,
> WE NEVER FORGET WHAT WE STAND FOR,
> WE NEVER FORGET WHY WE ARE HERE,
> FOR ALL YOU HAVE TO DO IS SIMPLY
> BELIEVE IT,
> AND YOU CAN ACHIEVE IT!!
> Thanks for a great season . . . . . . 95 lb. Coaches

🏈 🏈 🏈

"I think I like one of the cheerleaders," Stevie says. He and the rest of the Warriors wait in a corner of the Northwest Boys & Girls Club's home park. The 75-pounders are playing on the main field now, in a game preceding the 95s' last game of the season. A drizzle dampens Northwest's homecoming celebrations. A DJ spins R&B under a tarp canopy. Another clear plastic sheet covers a bank of speakers tall enough for an arena rock show. Falcons cheerleaders swing to a *thump-thump* that, because of the distorting tarp, may or may not be a song by Usher.

"Yo, yo, waz up?" Diamond asks Brian when the head coach checks in on the team. Games are running behind schedule on account of the rain. During the delay Diamond has, so far, consumed two pouches of fruit punch. As with Dr. Jekyll and his potion, Diamond's sugary drinks manifest themselves in an unusually animated personality. "This is our last game," he says, bouncing on his toes with every word. "We . . . gotta . . . shut . . . them . . . down. After the game, then we clown all we want."

Brian's eyes follow a trail of smoke rising from a barbecue grill, over the playing field, and up into a line of pine trees. The disappointment of the homecoming defeat remains on his mind. Although he acts nonchalant, the efforts by some fathers to oust him as head coach fail to roll off his back as easily as the rain drips off his black umbrella.

"If they thought they such wonderful coaches, why are they not out here?" Brian asks. "They can't take it, understand what I'm saying? I'm more of a man because I don't give a damn. I don't give a damn what nobody says. They can all say what they want to say, that we suck and we shouldn't be coaching and all, but I don't hear it. As long as blood is pumping in my veins you can't deter me. You can't deter me that easy, man."

In a parking lot next to the field, Luther Campbell shares an umbrella with Sam Johnson. The Baltimore Ravens jersey Campbell wears originally belonged to Ray Lewis, the Ravens linebacker and a University of Miami alum. Homespun philanthropist McAdoo hovers just outside the umbrella's protection, unbothered by the rain. As water dribbles off the bill of his baseball cap he tells Sam and Luther about his son's football future. He admits he's not exactly a hands-off father.

"My dream is through him," he crows. "Boom! All the things I ain't do right, I want him to do 'em right. He's at the position I love, linebacker. He's at the position I always wanted to play. He gonna wear the colors I love, the blue and gold of the Northwestern Bulls.

He going to take my dream and take it on out where I want to take it to, through him."

The 95s comandeer the field for a sloppy game. Running backs gain no yards, for either team. The rain-slicked ball slips from Antwane's fingers before he can finish his throwing motion. Not that his receivers run where they are supposed to; because of the rain, chalky yardage markers have dissolved into the mud. The Warriors fumble, the Falcons fumble, and the Warriors fumble again. The chocolate pudding playing field lends verisimilitude to the football term "pig pile." The final score is 7–6, Falcons.

"I love all y'all," eulogizes Coach Pete under the pine trees afterward. Diamond and Antwane peel off their dirty uniforms. "Y'all, in the future, want to come see me you can just come over. I enjoyed you all."

Because this is the last game of the season, the players hand over all their equipment, helmets and everything. Brian stuffs the wet jerseys into the mesh bag. The helmets are bulky and impossible to carry en masse, so Brian and Beasley make several trips to an equipment van rented by the Optimist Club.

After games the two coahces like to break down the Warriors' performance. Sometimes they spend hours on the phone discussing, in great detail, exactly what went wrong. Today there is no analysis. There is no talk of Georgia Southern, or of Antwane's inexplicable failure to learn the system. The two friends walk in silence from the pile of helmets to the van and back again. When the last of the equipment has been collected, Brian slides shut the van's side door.

"Come on," he says. "Let's get out of here before our name is mud."

"What do you mean 'before'?" asks Beasley. "Our name already *is* mud."

Chapter 16

Playoffs

Palmetto finished its regular season with a home win against Inner City, an untalented team from a park new to Pop Warner. Late in the game, the Raiders quarterback was struck on his blind side by an Inner City player; Campos insists the hit was a cheap shot. Tempers escalated. Several Inner City players and their parents rushed the Palmetto sideline. The father of Carl Martin, the Raiders' gifted running back, retrieved a gun from his car. He told Campos afterward that he will do whatever he must to protect himself.

"One of these days something is going to blow up at one of these games," Campos says. "I wonder if I'm in the right place. This league is full of thugs. It's getting out of control."

● ● ●

The Kendall Boys & Girls Club sits off an expressway named for Don Shula, the former coach of the Miami Dolphins. The club shares a parking lot with a Tony Roma's rib restaurant. Just before ten on a Sunday morning, a stream of pickup trucks and SUVs park in the lot. Men in khaki shorts, arms laden with folders, trudge from their trucks into the park's clubhouse. With the regular season wrapped up, it's time to select the seedings for the playoffs.

A children's activity room serves as tournament headquarters. Hippity Hops jockey for floor space with basketballs trapped in large wire bins. Several conference tables form a hollow square, around which sit the various park commissioners. A man in a Palmetto Raiders polo and hat. A three-man crew representing Suniland. Sam and Daryl from Liberty City. The commissioner of the Northwest Boys & Girls Club. Two men in Gwen Cherry Bulls gear, their hats, shirts, shorts, and Air Jordans all matching the blue-and-gold Bulls color scheme. Goulds Rams wear hats embroidered with their team logo, the same oval "G" worn by the University of Georgia. Everyone keeps his jacket buttoned against an air conditioner stuck on full blast.

Three boxes of donuts tempt from a side table, along with a half-gallon of milk and a dozen sixteen-ounce Styrofoam cups of coffee. "That's very nice, thank you," says Eric Stephens, the Suniland commissioner, as he grabs one of the warm cups.

Greater Miami Pop Warner director Mark Peterson calls the meeting to order. He pulls from his satchel a couple of sheets of crinkled white paper. "I did these until the middle of the night," he says, glancing at the brackets, resetting a blue Pop Warner baseball cap atop his disheveled hair. A crayon left over from day care rolls off the table onto the checkerboard floor. On a bulletin board behind Peterson, finger-painted pumpkins and ghosts dance in advance of Halloween.

"In the 95s, the winners are Gwen Cherry, Palmetto, and Overtown. The wild cards go to Goulds, Richmond, and Northwest Boys Club." Sam Johnson grimaces at the finality of it. Brian's Liberty City 95s are out.

At other weight levels, Liberty City represents better. The Warriors 110s and 125s have earned spots in the playoffs, and will be hosting games. The 145-pound Warriors are in too, though who they will be playing is still up in the air. Palmetto 145s head coach Raul Campos, through his park commissioner, has filed a protest against the Richmond Giants. Campos has been sitting on his box of evidence all season, reams of paper documenting, supposedly, how the Giants defeated the Raiders in the season opener with players who either were too old or were ineligible school dropouts. In lobbying for Richmond's suspension, Campos insisted, through his commissioner, that the Giants were "nothing but a bunch of thugs."

"Calling them 'thugs,' he might as well have been calling them 'niggers,'" says Liberty City's Daryl Hence. "He made me want to beat him down myself. He done lost my respect."

The timing of the complaint doesn't sit well with Mark Peterson. If there was any merit to Campos's protest he should have brought it up earlier—say, three months earlier. Request denied. Richmond stays in the playoffs as the winner of its division. Goulds and Overtown are the other division winners. Palmetto sneaks in with a wild card. The Raiders will play Florida City at home on Wednesday.

🏈 🏈 🏈

U.S. Flags, where Mark Peterson works, is a small business. The company's storefront blends into a strip of warehouses on the outskirts of The Falls, one of Miami's better shopping malls. To the north, an indoor batting cage helps teenagers improve their softball swings. Across the street an auto body shop unbends fenders. A neighboring store sells roller-hockey skates and sticks. Peterson's is the easiest company to find. Just look for the giant flagpole.

Peterson sits at a small wooden desk next to another desk occupied by his mother, who handles drop-in visitors. Peterson's father sits a desk over. His brother works in the back room. Most every day, for most of all day, the three Petersons up front man the phones, which never stop ringing. Since September 11 so many orders have come in for flags or, even more profitably, for construction of the kind of large, freestanding flagpoles often seen in front of schools, that the Petersons are hustling to meet demand. It's a rush of business they are as grateful for as they are uneasy about, considering the circumstances behind the boom.

Peterson's grandfather started U.S. Flags seventy-five years ago, in New Jersey. When the family moved the business to Miami twenty years ago, Peterson attempted to strike out on his own, as a landscaper. Hurricane Andrew blew away his nursery, and his independence. He's been helping to run the flag business ever since. Two or three times a week, Peterson crosses Dixie Highway to eat lunch at a strip-mall deli. He's usually accompanied by his father. During lunch, work is never discussed. Every year as Halloween approaches, Peterson finds himself talking about football.

"This is the time of year when people show their true colors," he says, settling into his seat at the deli. "Come late October and early November, for the playoffs, we see what people are all about. All year long they're usually polite and respectful and magnanimous and talk about how they're all about the kids and so forth. But come playoff time, then they all drop their masks."

Campos's conspiracy theories concerning Richmond amuse Peterson. In a way. Here is a coach whose questionable practices, along with those of Gator Rebhan at Suniland, necessitated the drafting of rules to prevent migration of talent from one park to another; Peterson feels there's something funny about a guy like this complaining about the ethics of another program. Yet the emphasis on winning that Campos, Rebhan, and coaches of their ilk embody is something the director is finding increasingly difficult to combat.

Problems associated with sports at the college level have drifted down to high school programs in Miami. Northwestern and Jackson have been caught changing grades of their star players to make them eligible during football season. The schools keep them enrolled just long enough to play out the season, then let them drop out to face the world without even the thin protection of a diploma. State officials dismantled the dynastic basketball team at Miami Senior High after catching boosters lending addresses to star players who lived outside the school's attendance boundaries.

Such cheating has started drifting down further, to youth sports. Fake birth certificates, waivers for kids flunking out of school. There is recruiting, definitely. Kids are being used to further . . .

". . . the goals of the adults," Peterson says, carrying out the thought to its logical conclusion. "And that's the problem. We're supposed to be teaching these kids something, yet what some of these coaches or adults are teaching is that it's okay to be bought, it's okay not to do well in school because you're going to play for me anyway because you're a stud, you're a superstar. By the time these kids get to high school, I'm telling you, that mind-set is ingrained in them."

Peterson chomps into a chicken salad sandwich. He sips his iced tea. From his seat near the window he can see the lights that illuminate night games at Suniland Park.

"That's my problem with Campos," he says. "He's not teaching these kids anything about what they should be. He's only teaching them how to win. You gotta also learn how to lose. And he doesn't do it. He better hope for his sake that they do go to Orlando, or he'll have a problem to contend with."

*   *   *

Only half the teams from Palmetto made the playoffs, so there is more room than usual at practice for Campos to run his offense through the Florida City game plan. The defense drops into the four-point stance for assistant coach Lee. Another coach drills the offensive line, using his arms to demonstrate a chop block. Campos and the skill players jog onto the main field to practice under lights illuminating a fading dusk.

He proceeds through the usual paces, calling out the same plays some of these boys have been practicing for three years. Sweeps and power runs straight up the middle. Option passes to streaking wide receivers. Each play works every time, an endorsement of rote repetition. The quarterback throws a fake pitch to a running back, pivots, then passes to a wide receiver slashing toward midfield.

"There we go! In the house! In the house, bay bee!" shouts Carl's father, the one with the gun.

Jarmaine Brockington, resting between plays, shifts his weight from one leg to the other. Boxer shorts more than peek out the top of his pants, which, for intentional fashion purposes, he lets hang below the crack of his buttocks. A gold ring shines on his left pinky. Gold bracelets as thin as thread jangle on his left wrist. Soft, short dreads sprout from his scalp like strings on a mop. He watches an assistant coach throw a beautiful spiral forty yards downfield. A receiver runs to catch the ball, his legs blurring in a display of pure speed.

Before the playoff seedings were announced, the Raiders assumed Richmond would be removed from the playoffs. An assistant coach guaranteed several players that they were on the fast track to Orlando. "We're going to Disney, baby. It's a done deal," he said before the last game. Now that Richmond remains in the playoffs—along with Overtown, another team that defeated Palmetto this season—victory isn't so assured. Campos is trying to move on.

"It bothers me, but some things you gotta put away," he says as he watches the offense practice. "If you let it bother you it will get in the way of your coaching, and you can't let it do that. I've got to focus myself to help these kids in the proper way and get them ready for that game."

Campos has been coaching in Miami since 1979, at several different parks. When he arrived at Palmetto fifteen years ago, the park was exclusively white. He shepherded change by bringing in good black players and coaches, just as he had done at other parks where he'd coached. He also brought a swagger to Palmetto never before seen in youth sports. He rented a fleet of limos to pick up his players on the field after every win. Together they'd drive to a steak house, where he'd treat them to dinner. Sponsors – his construction buddies – would pick up the tab.

"I was the first one to come out with the warm-up jackets," he says. "I was the first one to come up with two different-colored jerseys for home and away. Nobody had them before. We have the pirate mascot and the DJs spinning music after the games. Now, if I get off my ass and find sponsors, why not? These kids would never have nothing like this in their lives."

The favors he uses to attract great athletes to his program fuel his success more than any of his self-described offensive genius. Resentment at losing to him every year inspired Suniland and other parks to offer similar inducements to players. Gator Rebhan's players at Suniland received letter jackets and fat gold rings after their

Super Bowl win. The cost of winning in Pop Warner football is escalating.

"They're letting all this animosity build," Campos asserts. Though he's referring to Richmond's rogue team, he might as well be talking about the hostility he personally introduced to the league. "Everyone wants to make it to the playoffs. Everyone wants to go to nationals. They're letting this thing get out of hand. Boy, one of these days, man, this shit is going to blow up and somebody's going to get shot. Watch."

🏈 🏈 🏈

Three hours before kickoff, an assistant coach named Brown tends to a crop of thin, flexible aluminum wires he has planted behind the west end zone. The tips of the dozen or so wires stick into the ground at six-foot intervals, creating an archway over which Brown drapes black plastic garbage bags. The plan is to build a tunnel for the Raiders to run through prior to kickoff. It's hard work tying the bags down. And, once secured, the contraption is vulnerable to a strengthening breeze darting across Palmetto Field. Brown ditched his job at a day care center to build the tunnel. He's been here for two and a half hours already.

Campos pulls up in his SUV. Jarmaine exits the passenger side. When Campos spies the listing tunnel, he phones another assistant with an order of duct tape and twine. He also calls his wife Gloria and asks her to bring out twenty-seven black-and-silver Raider flags and the pirate's uniform for the mascot to wear: knee-length black boots, a ruffled shirt, an overcoat, knickers, and a sword to tuck into a wide black belt.

"If we're going to do it, might as well do it in style," he says after he flips shut his phone.

Campos stalks off to the berm. He sits on an overturned milk crate, strokes his beard, and visualizes his game plan. One by one, over the course of the next hour, he is joined by assistant coaches. Coach Lee. Coach Willy. The team commissioner. Campos called

Lee late last night to talk over some plays. He called Willy at two in the morning to pepper him with hypothetical situations about the offensive line. He wants his coaches thinking about the game like he is.

"Hey," he says. "I do my homework, man."

Players begin arriving, joining Jarmaine in a loose circle. Two players wear black letter jackets Campos bought them.

"Too many people came up to me today and say, 'You gonna lose,'" says Milton, a slender offensive lineman with the letter "J" tattooed onto his bicep. Another player talks about the betting line. "When we lost to Overtown, this guy says he lost fifteen hundred dollars. I saw someone out here yesterday says he has twelve hundred dollars on this game."

At 6 P.M. the bell tower atop a nearby church chimes out a request for peace on earth. The coach of the 110s, who will be playing Goulds in the opener, places orange foam markers on the corners of the end zones. Yellow pillows mark the yard lines. The goalposts are wrapped in black foam. A cameraman sets up video equipment in a press box above the bleachers. Campos and his assistants change into their white shirts and black ties.

Night falls, bringing with it the Florida City Razorbacks, who confiscate stretching space near the playing field. Florida City's players form a circle around a blue Chevy Malibu painted iridescent blue. The car's backseat has been removed and replaced by a door-to-door woofer, a speaker that vibrates a Trina rap. With the car and the music the Razorbacks strut as if they are the home team, a play ripped from Campos's unpublished autobiography. If the strategy unnerves Campos a little, he says nothing. He does veto the mascot. And he tells his wife to keep the twenty-seven Raider flags in her car.

The Palmetto 110s win in overtime, just as the humidity coalesces into a quick shower. A growing crowd on the bleachers puffs clouds of marijuana smoke into the moist night. The Florida City cheerleaders stand, hands on hips, on the visiting sideline. Campos's wife hands orange slices to any Raiders who want one.

"Clap it up! Clap it up!"

"Break it down! Break it down!"

A generator roars to life, powering the smoke machine. A white cloud rises from the tunnel. Behind the cloud flow the Palmetto Raiders 145s, aspiring national champions. Coach Campos leads the charge.

"If we lose we out," Campos says to his players while the captains meet at midfield for the coin toss. "This is a rivalry game, but I'm telling you, Florida City is nothing. They know we beat them already. Ain't nobody can beat Palmetto. All right—hands in, let's go. Raiders on three."

Campos is right: Florida city is nothing. Although the Razorbacks carry a lead into halftime, they crumble in the second half. Costly fumbles are converted into Raider touchdowns. The final score of 24–14 makes the game seem closer than it actually was.

"It was a shoot-out," says Campos afterward, shouting to be heard over the Palmetto crowd. "I think both sides fired their guns, but we came out on top."

The Malibu that arrived with the Florida City team tricks a wide donut in the Raiders' practice field. The driver of the car fires three pistol shots toward the berm and the grocery store parking lot behind it. No one is hit or injured. The police are not called.

Chapter 17

Palmetto vs. Goulds

If a pop quiz were assigned to the nation, and one of the questions was "What is the bird most associated with Miami?" almost everyone would answer the flamingo. The fragile pink birds with long, backward-bending straws for legs. Publicity-loving supermodels with graceful necks and plumage stained pink by an iodine-heavy shrimp diet.

In Miami, people taking the quiz would know better. Flamingos may be the bird pushed by the tourism folks, but, outside of the zoo, Parrot Jungle, and the infield of the Hialeah horse track, the bird can't be found anywhere. A far more common bird flies down from Ohio every October to roost on the county courthouse ziggurat. This bird winters on heat waves rising over downtown parking lots. Lunch is fresh offerings from the Dinner Key landfill. The turkey vulture is a mascot as appropriate for Miami as it is familiar, an opportunistic scavenger here for the sun and the garbage and the dead bodies floating in Biscayne Bay.

Turkey vultures appear in earnest on the last Saturday in October. As if it were a prearranged welcome back, the weather finally breaks. For the first time since late March the temperature tops out at just 70 degrees. Air conditioners rest. Windows open. Boaters floating down the river wear sweaters instead of bikini tops. A Miami winter has arrived at last, bringing to sun-deranged residents the same exhilaration someone in Vermont feels at the first sign of spring.

"Where God guides he provides! Do I have a witness! Sanctify!" Two hours before the semifinal game between Palmetto and the Goulds Rams, the cooling breeze carries over Goulds Field the gospel of an evangelist. The sermon passes from a Baptist church to soccer fields, basketball courts, and the rippling surface of an empty public swimming pool. Cheerleaders not yet in uniform practice their routines. The first Goulds Ram players drag in, their shoulder pads and helmets slung over their shoulders. A man staples flyers to trees advertising the Miss Gusto swimsuit competition. "Bring the body and the swimsuit for a chance to win a thousand dollars cash." A few cars claim prime tailgating spots.

"We won! We won!" Little boys stretch out the windows of a yellow school bus rolling into the park. The 95-pound Rams—the team that defeated Liberty City in the first game of the season—are returning from a road game in which they earned a place in next week's city championships. The Palmetto 145s cruise in right behind the Rams' bus. Palmetto Field is located only three miles from Goulds Field. Yet the Raiders again arrive not in their own cars, nor in a banal yellow school bus; Campos has chartered his usual deluxe motor coach, a bus featuring tinted windows, plush seats, television monitors, and a bathroom. Goulds Rams stare at the cruiser in awe. The Palmetto coaches descend in their ties, white shirts, and black pants. Assistant coach Lee covers his uniform with his black leather Palmetto letterman jacket, just like the players wear, the model with two national championship patches sewn on the sleeves.

"Damn!" says one Ram to his friend.

Although a few coaches have left the bus, Campos and the players stay onboard for forty more minutes. It's a mind game, he admits. Campos wants everyone at the park to stare at his shiny motor coach and wonder what is happening inside.

"There's a lot of animosity between Goulds and me," he says from his seat in the first row. "I coached there for two years. They didn't want me to leave, but it was impossible to coach there. It's a circus. We were 7–1 and we were still being called assholes and motherfuckers and everything else because we were losing one game that we eventually won. So now they hate me. I mean, they can't stand me."

When the Raiders finally exit the bus, players pull on their pads. Most wear low-slung pants without hip pads, which are deemed unfashionable. A linebacker hands diamond earrings to an assistant coach. The studs disappear into the pocket of the coach's jacket, next to a few more earrings and a snake pit of thick platinum necklaces. Another coach ducks into the bus's luggage bin to retrieve a tank of compressed oxygen, a perk Campos provides his players.

League commissioner Mark Peterson arrives just before kickoff. He mans the gate in the north end zone, making sure no one comes onto the field who shouldn't be there. Sitting next to him on a lawn chair is the vice president of the league, a volunteer from predominantly white Coral Park. Peterson, who failed to anticipate the plunging thermometer, hunches his shoulders inside his denim jacket.

"Damn, it's cold!" he huffs.

By now more than a thousand people have arrived at the park. When Liberty City played Goulds in the opening week of the season, a droopy yellow rope separated fans from the playing field. In the weeks since that game the rope has been replaced by a chain-link fence, theoretically for better security. With fans three and four deep all the way around the field, the security fence more closely resembles a cage used in a wrestling match. The bleachers on both sides of the field sag with spectator weight. A few fans behind the Palmetto bench openly support the Raiders. Most everyone else has chosen to watch the game from this vantage point to be near Campos, the head coach they so despise.

"No more recruiting, no more recruiting!" chants a man wearing a baseball hat colored Rams red and gray. "You better go back to coaching the 75s, Campos. It's going to be an ugly game."

Adults place their hands atop the fence and peer over, five hundred Kilroys ready for action. Young boys squint through diamonds in the chain. A few acrobats balance on top of the fence, taunting the arriving Raiders from their perch.

"The pirate ship is going down today!"

"One first down all day long!"

Beyond the south end zone, where the rapper Trick Daddy has parked his lime green Chevy Impala, more than two hundred men—and they are all men—stand in orange knit caps and sweatshirts with hoods pulled over their heads. They drink from paper bags, smoke blunts, and lay their bets. Rooting for the home Rams is one thing; wagering on them is another matter altogether.

"I'm going with the gray and black, yes sir," says one fan, placing his cash on Campos and the Raiders.

One Rams fan on the Palmetto bleachers taps an air horn so frequently he may as well be sending Morse code. It's annoying the hell out of the Raider coaches and players, exactly as the man intends.

"Oh, I'm a hata!" he cackles when asked to shut up. "I'm a Raida . . . playa . . . hata!" He repeats his chant, taping the air horn after every word. The animosity toward Palmetto is high. It only rises after Goulds scores first to take an 8–0 lead.

"It over! It over! It over!" chants the crowd, by now a thousand voices united. The bleachers shake dangerously. The ground vibrates as feet land after ecstatic leaps. On the Palmetto bench, Campos struggles to maintain control over a team with an impulse to collapse. Even his coaches are at each other's throats.

"The O line is not blockin'," complains Coach Brown.

"Don't blame it on me!" spits back Coach Willy, who oversees the line.

"Get focused!" commands Coach Lee. "We gonna win."

The Raiders offense fails to sustain a drive. Three straight plays generate only nine yards, leaving Campos with fourth-and-one deep in his own territory. Goulds fans familiar with Campos's coaching style talk trash.

"Uh-oh, Campos," taunts a Rams fan. "You better punt. Be smart. Punt the ball. We know you don't punt, but you better punt now."

Campos decides not to punt, as his reputation dictates. It's a bad decision: Running back Jarmaine Brockington is stuffed for a major loss. Rams ball. Campos clasps his hands behind his head in exasperation, or perhaps to shield himself from the shower of cackles thrown by the crowd. The score remains 8–0 at halftime.

"These niggas need heart," grumbles a Palmetto fan. Jarmaine, as he did at halftime of the Overtown loss, sits on the bench apart from the team, his hands clasped, elbows on his knees, head down, eyes studying the orange dirt of the baseball diamond beneath him. His purple mouthpiece dangles from his mask. He rips the tape from his cleats, a signal that he's quit.

"What we all got going for us is they played the best half of their lives and we only down 8–0," Campos advises. "And we stunk up the place. All we have to do is play half as good as they did and we'll win, easy."

"Campos can't win," crows the Rams fan with the air horn. "I don't care what you say, he can't come back. It over with. Campos can't come back in this one." The man administers a horn blast. "I'm a Raida hata, oh yeah!"

The floodlights spark to life to start the second half. The crowd continues to thicken, with late arrivals doubling the number of fans piled around the fence. The taunting grows more spirited. So do the Raiders. Carl, at running back, gains thirty yards in a single play. On a fourth down, Bryan, at quarterback, throws up a "dying quail," a wobbly pass that floats for so long in the gray clouds that Campos has time to ask Randall, the intended receiver, to forget about trying to catch the ball and just concentrate on preventing the Rams from intercepting it.

"Randall! Knock it down!" Campos hollers. Randall doesn't knock it down. Instead he leaps high enough to dunk a basketball. As his feet are kicked out from under him, his entire body parallel to his defender's red helmet, he catches the ball. Four plays later Palmetto scores a touchdown and makes it 8–8, the score at the end of regulation time.

"Whooee! We believe it! We believe it!" a Palmetto coach cries. "The best defense in Pop Warner here. Shut 'em down now. Let's go! It's not over."

Like they do in college football, Miami Pop Warner uses the Kansas tie-breaker system. One team gets the ball on the 10-yard line and has four opportunities, or downs, to score either a touchdown or a field goal. The other team then gets the ball on the 10-yard line and its own set of downs. If the second team scores more points, it wins; if it scores fewer points, it loses. If the score remains tied they start over, going round after round until one team finally wins.

Palmetto tries first. Jarmaine, back in the game now that the Raiders are back to life, gains nine yards on first down, setting up a certain touchdown. Except the Raiders fail to score on second down. And then on third down. Conventional wisdom dictates that Campos attempt a field goal to at least put some points on the scoreboard. Instead he goes for a touchdown. And he fails. Goulds ball. All the Rams need do is kick a field goal. A few Goulds fans leap over the fence in anticipation of the certain win.

"As soon as they score, everybody else over the fence," one of them says. "We gonna tear down those goalposts."

Needing only a field goal, Goulds plays conservatively. Two running plays up the middle actually lose a yard, leading to third and eleven. A penalty on Palmetto makes it third and six. A subsequent run gains nothing, though it really doesn't matter. The Goulds kicker trots on the field for an easy field goal try.

"Oh, shit!" mutters Coach Willy. "Block that kick! Block that kick! Block that kick!"

And the Raiders do. Palmetto lives for another round.

A football overtime never has to end. If every touchdown by one team is matched by a touchdown by the other, the process starts over again. Same thing if both teams miss their field goal tries. The expectation is that one team, finally, will score more points than the other, though that's not at all guaranteed. Palmetto and Goulds seem eager to prove this point. The Raiders fail to score with their next four downs. Goulds, again poised for certain victory, promptly fumbles the ball back to Palmetto. Fans itching to tear down the goalposts scurry back over the fence like roaches caught in a suddenly illuminated kitchen.

There's an old adage in sports: You've got to knock out the champ when he's down. Goulds has blown two perfect opportunities to win the game. Palmetto is too strong, too athletic, too talented to stay out of the end zone much longer. Raul Campos, with his motor coach and his oxygen tanks and his goddamn black tie and black pants and sorry-ass team, is going back to the city championships. It's all but certain. As the Palmetto quarterback steps behind his center, the malice toward Campos and his team is palpable, metallic. The quarterback checks his receivers, checks the defensive formation, then barks out his commands.

Pop! Pop!

The sound of the gun, when fired, is not in and of itself menacing. One sharp, clean snap, then another. Friendly fire if it weren't for the volume, which is so loud, coming from behind the Palmetto bleachers, that everyone in the park reacts instinctively. Fans, players, coaches, and referees dive to the ground. All lie on their stomachs, hands over their ears, heads rising just enough for eyes to scan the bleachers.

"Is anyone hit?"

"I can't see nothing, man."

"That was a gun, right?"

"Damn right that was a gun!"

"What happened?"

"Just shut up, boy! How the fuck I know?"

Five seconds. Six, seven. Ten. Like zombies escaping marshy graves, all rise. The players in their armor, the fans stacked in cords along the fence, the coaches with clods of brown dirt stuck on their white oxfords. A linesman dusts off his striped cap. Raiders look at Rams. What the fuck's going on?

"It's over! It is OVER!" shouts a large black man in a red windbreaker that indicates he works at the county park. He has leaped the chain-link fence. He is marching purposefully toward the head referee. He is waving his arms across his chest like an umpire signaling a base runner safe at home. "This game is OVER! No more! This game is over! You have gunshots fired. Gunshots mean 'OVER.' No more. Game over! The game is *over!*"

The man, a bureaucrat with liability issues, is making the safe call. If there are gunshots, he continues, the game must end. He's acting instinctively, of course, and on paper his decision makes solid sense. But this is the playoffs. And the winner goes to the city championship. And it's quadruple overtime. When you call a game that has grown this important, and at this crucial a point in that game, the last thing you are doing, ironically, is maintaining safety.

"What?!?" The veins on Campos's neck throb. His forehead and his cheeks explode in crimson pyrotechnics. His eyes bulge. The voice he uses to shout his disagreement with the ruling is louder than the gunshots. The Goulds head coach joins the protest, united with Campos for once: "Ain't no way you calling this."

"You not putting that responsibility in my hands," the administrator shouts back as the coaches circle him. "You have gunshots, game over. Fuck that, man."

The referee, feeling powerless to challenge the bureaucrat, calls the game. Every coach on both teams surround him so quickly, and with threats of violence so real, the ref's skin drains of color. He backpedals toward midfield. Fans toss hats and cans and glass bottles onto the pitch. Gits leaping the fence thicken the mob circling the lone referee. Ignored in the sea of bodies and screaming coaches and irate fans is the sight, just beyond the bleachers, of two county cops wrestling a man's face into the orange dirt of a baseball diamond.

The man, a 19-year-old student, will be charged with firing his gun in a public place. The police incident report will not reveal the shooter's motivation. Most of the crowd already knows the answer: He had his money on Goulds. And when Goulds fumbled away a victory, placing his stake in serious jeopardy, he shot two bullets toward the sky in an attempt to stop the game.

As the police deal with the shooter, Mark Peterson runs to the ref's assistance. He pulls him away from the growing mob, away especially from Campos, who continues to shout and wave his arms in an anger that has short-circuited his normally careful control. With Peterson protecting the ref, Campos stalks back to his sideline.

"If they call this game we win!" the Raiders' head coach tells his team. He scribbles out a game plan on a dry-erase board, should the game continue. His players, watching Peterson huddle with the referee and the park worker, hopped up on adrenaline from the game and the gunshots, are too excited to watch the plays being diagrammed. "Hey!" Campos shouts to get their attention. "Hey! Hey!" The veins in his neck are thick and round as pencils. "Shut the fuck up already."

In the huddle at midfield, Mark Peterson pacifies the park administrator. Peterson is reasonable. Like the park man, he would like to drive away from this game right now, back to his family, back to his flag business. As league commissioner, he faces liability issues of his own. Peterson and the head referee agree that, since no one got hit by the bullets, and since two thousand amped-up fans, many of them drunk and/or stoned, would riot if the game were canceled, it's safest to play it out.

"I'd hate to see someone get shot out here," Peterson says. A county police officer in the huddle counters that it would be ludicrous to play on, and argues for the game's immediate cancellation. He is overruled by Peterson and the head referee, who is also a county cop, off duty. The ref gets his police car and parks it between the hash marks on the 40-yard line (in overtime they don't use the whole field). He turns on his lights to send a disco ball of red and white dots racing across the field and the bleachers and the backs of the linebackers, who are still wondering if the game will be played out.

"I got a shotgun back there," the ref says as he exits his squad car. He points to his backseat. "I got six hundred forty rounds. No one in the crowd is better armed than me. I could take down everyone here if I have to. I'm serious. I got more firepower than anyone."

When play finally resumes, Palmetto scores the go-ahead touchdown, as everyone expected. The extra point is good. Goulds needs to score a touchdown and an extra point or Palmetto advances to the city championship. On the Rams' first attempt to tie, Goulds' best running back is stopped, buckles his knee, and is carted off the field. Goulds fails to score on second or third down, either. It has come down to one last chance. One play to tie it or to send Palmetto to the championship. The referee approaches Mark Peterson, who's sitting on the front bumper of the squad car.

"We're not sticking around for the handshake," he tells the commissioner. "That's all yours." The ref also approaches Campos. "Coach, I just want to say that if you guys win, congratulations. I'm not sticking around when this ends."

Logistically, things would be easier if the Rams don't score a touchdown. But they do. However, the elation expressed by the Goulds fans—fresh life, another chance to win—is painfully short-lived. The same Rams kicker who earlier missed two easy field goals shanks his extra-point attempt. The ball grazes the outside of the right goalpost—no good. Palmetto wins the semifinal playoff game. Palmetto, and Coach Campos, are in the city championship. Raider coaches stream onto the field to hug their players. The ref bolts for his car, pealing away so quickly he leaves skid marks at midfield.

"Y'all champions!" shouts Coach Brown. Coach Lee points his index finger skyward: Palmetto is number one. One Raiders player tosses a football high into the night. His teammates track the arc of the ball with whistles, as if the ball were a grenade. When it hits the turf, everyone shouts "Boom!" while collapsing as if hit by shrapnel.

"On the bus!" commands Campos. "Let's go. Get the gear! Let's go!"

Jarmaine Brockington strips off his equipment. His brother, Trick Daddy, hands him a wad of cash, a reward for a game well-played, even if he did quit at halftime. An assistant hands back

Jarmaine's jewelry: a pair of earrings and a platinum rope, which the boy throws around his neck.

"Nobody would believe when we lost to Richmond that we would be back. Nobody wanted to believe that we could retaliate, but we did," says a linebacker named Javon. "We dangerous."

The driver of a car stuck in traffic calls out to Campos: "It's all about the black and gray, and we love that green!" The driver reaches out to shake Campos's hand. "We love it!"

Campos runs the fingers of his free hand through his hair, which is wet with water from the cooler. He removes his tie and unbuttons his oxford shirt so he can change into a dry T-shirt for the ride back home.

"This is the second time this year there was a shooting at Goulds," he says. "If I were to tell anyone about this, that there were shots fired and there was a police car on the fifty-yard line with the lights flashing and we still continued the game—they wouldn't believe me. If this were anywhere else in the country this shit'd be on the six o'clock news. Here I bet you anything you don't even hear about it."

The shooting goes unreported by every local television station. There is no mention of the incident in the newspaper the next day. The city championships proceed as scheduled.

Chapter 18

Voting

Maurice Ferre served as Miami's mayor in the early seventies, before Cuban exiles altered Miami's political landscape. Ferre's political career is checkered with achievements and embarrassments, same as just about every other Miami politician. Mostly he is remembered as the last mayor with a big-picture vision for developing the city. He launched the movement to land a basketball team and baseball team. Ferre personally recruited architect I. M. Pei to design what has become the city's signature skyscraper.

The current mayor, Joe Carollo, killed his chances at reelection by throwing a box of tea at his wife, who'd sued him for divorce. (The incumbent hit her so violently his ten-year-old daughter dialed 911.) Carollo finished third in the November 5 primary, out of the runoff. The two remaining candidates are Ferre and Manny Diaz, the Cuban attorney and political neophyte who was part of the Elián Gonzalez legal team. In an endorsement for Ferre, the black-owned *Miami Times* noted, "Diaz is spending more money than any other candidate, but this community remembers him as the lawyer for the Elián fiasco that almost destroyed this city. There is a strong feeling in this community that Cuban elected officials have been insensitive to the point of arrogance in their relationship with blacks."

In the week between the primary and the runoff, Diaz supporters flood Spanish language radio stations with phone calls tying

Ferre to former attorney general Janet Reno, the woman who authorized the abduction of Elián from the home of his Miami relatives. Ferre had said in a television interview that he would *not* back her possible campaign for governor, but Diaz's supporters twisted those words to make it sound as if Ferre had actually supported Reno, an act of political suicide, had it been true.

The day before the election, Diaz eats a lunch of chicken salad at the Versailles restaurant, a meeting place for Cuban politicians. He also rides around Little Havana on a pickup truck, waving at his loyal Cuban constituents. Ferre, for his part, casts his lot with a coalition of blacks and non-Hispanic whites, or "Anglos" as they are referred to in Miami. He joins a motorcade through all-black Overtown and Liberty City and through ethnically mixed Allapattah, with its blacks and non-Cuban Hispanics. Ferre returns to Liberty City to eat lunch at a Veterans Day barbecue.

Election Day, November 13, is warm and humid. Bayberry dust floating in a stiff wind raises the pollen count. At Hadley Park, voting booths are set up in a community room next to the pool. In the winter darkness one hour before the polls close, volunteers remain outside the park gate. These "volunteers" are usually paid for their support, $50 or so to hold a candidate's sign. A white van with a megaphone attached to its roof rolls slowly past.

"Punch number eighty-three for Maurice Ferre, he is best for our community," intones the driver. "Eighty-three is the number. Eighty-three is the number and Ferre is the candidate."

When the polls close at seven o'clock, the van steers downtown to the Wyndham Hotel, parking among a fleet of similar white vans. Inside the hotel, in a ballroom, platters of cubed cheese wait on silver trays. Members of a salsa band moisten trombone mouthpieces in anticipation of a victory party. A dozen men stand in the lobby with their ears to cell phones, monitoring early returns. A double-digit Ferre lead, someone shouts. A landslide victory, it appears. The band's lead singer tunes her voice.

The excitement lasts a few minutes at least. Once the votes in Little Havana start rolling in, the mood changes. Less than one hour after the polls close, Diaz stands outside the Orange Bowl in Little Havana absorbing the congratulations of his supporters, who rhythmically chant his name. Seventy-one percent of Cubans voted for Diaz, and way more Cubans voted than any other demographic group. Almost nine out of ten blacks voted for Ferre. Sixty-eight percent of Anglos, the city's smallest ethnic bloc, also voted for Ferre. Without the Cuban vote, though, he had no chance.

"I think what . . . keeps popping out is Elián and Janet Reno and, you know, the right-wing fanaticism in the Cuban-American community," Ferre told the *New York Times* the next morning. "It is the lockstep, blind, fanatical rejection of anything not within the purview of what they think is right. There is no middle ground in the minds of many of these people."

To local reporters, Ferre said much the same thing: "You cannot get away from the nationalism and the way the Cuban community feels. You cannot get away from the deep hurt in the Cuban community. Someday we'll live in a city where race, religion, and national orientation won't make a difference. Today they do. They played the nationalist card, and they played it effectively."

Ferre added that he had run his last race, that he was out of politics forever. Ferre's campaign manager threw out a quote with ramifications felt far beyond city hall.

"In this town," he said, "if you're not Cuban, you're nothing."

Chapter 19

City Championship

On the Friday before the city championships, a tropical storm named Michelle upgrades to a compact and powerful category-three hurricane. The executive director of the South Florida Water Management District assesses possible flooding. Local television news departments drop reports on anthrax outbreaks in favor of the threat they know best. Meteorologist Roland Steadham on WTVJ-TV (NBC 6) breathlessly reminds viewers that the storm, as of right now, is headed over the mountains of Cuba and is not going to hit Florida, much less Miami—but that could change. And as it is a hurricane with 111-mile-per hours winds, it has the potential to kill thousands of people.

"I'm not saying that it will in this case," Steadham reassuringly adds.

Because of such scare tactics, office workers wrap their computers in plastic bags before heading home for the weekend. A few overly paranoid homeowners cover their windows with plywood. It's impossible to find water or bread on the shelves at the supermarket behind Palmetto Field. The wind whipping across the field at practice is strong enough to curve extra-point attempts wide left. The 145s are the only Palmetto team still in the playoffs, so they have the whole field to themselves. The visiting bleachers have been carted away. The fence surrounding the field has been torn down until next season. The Raider players wear only shirts and shorts as they walk through the "quick game" ball-control offense Campos has prepared for the championship. The roster of nickel-and-dime passes—nothing too long—will work well if it rains tomorrow, which it isn't supposed to do.

The team is down to twenty-one players now. A receiver named Jamie was cut after the Goulds game, for his bad attitude. Nightmare was cut too, for his similarly bad outlook, according to Campos. It's technically against the rules to run off the problem players, yet Campos has a history of doing so. His most recent national championship team carried only eighteen players to Orlando; the teams he played fielded full squads of thirty-five. While at the professional or college level having more players is an advantage, at the youth level, with its rules of mandatory play, fewer players means more playing time for the superstars.

A player named Jeff stands on the sidelines in shorts and shiny blue Nike basketball shoes. He is not dressed for practice. He says his knee is hurting him. An assistant coach with the unlikely nickname Big Momma looks over at Jeff, and at his allegedly bum knee.

"Coach Lee call me at four in the morning, saying, 'Coach, Coach, I got us a linebacker,'" Big Momma says as he recalls the night Jeff signed with the Raiders. "That's one call I wish I never got," he tells the boy. "I should take you out to the pasture and shoot your ass dead because you're lame to us now."

Jeff is a freshman at Southridge High, a football power. He'd prefer to play ball for his school but he scored a bad grade in math and lost his eligibility. So he signed with the Raiders and one last season of Pop Warner ball. It was his best offer.

"The way I see it, Campos like a Rockefeller," he says. "I heard he's like the richest coach in Pop Warner." Jeff insists Campos uses his money to buy his team. Disney World, the jackets, the oxygen tank at games—"Those are bribes right there!" Jeff says. "You don't see Richmond riding in on no bus. That's a bribe right there, too."

* * *

Because of the weather, because of the slender victory over Goulds, and because of his inability to scrounge together $13,000, Campos postponed for yet another year his plan to deliver the Raiders to the city championships via helicopter. The players reluctantly motor in on their usual custom bus, pushing past cars with soaped-up windows and Raider flags flapping on antennas. Campos contemplates his strategy. Short passes. Ball control. He's a big believer in focusing on the task at hand. Yet during the week, even while he prepared to play for the city championship, he was also looking ahead. He made plans with one of his construction buddies to fly him and Coach Lee to Port Charlotte to scout the Hornets, their likely opponents in the state finals.

"We're 9–2," he told the team at the end of the last practice. "To some that's the best year they ever had. To us it's a bad season. Actually, it's not that bad—everyone else finished with two losses as well. But still they wrote us off. They wrote us off at the beginning of the season, but we knew we'd be back. It's our year yet again. If we win then we play Naples, then we play in Jacksonville for the state finals, then it's a week in Disney World."

At the mention of Disney World, everyone cheered.

Curtis Park, the site of the city championships, is an expansive field buffeted on three sides by strip malls and gas stations. On the south side freighters float down the Miami River past bridges locked down for the hurricane, just in case. The storm broke up over Cuba last night, as predicted. Whatever rain and wind that remains has angled off to the Bahamas. The ramifications in Miami are limited to an increase of surfers riding waves off Miami Beach. Clouds circle overhead, but as the Raiders' cruiser rolls into the lot, rain has yet to fall.

Campos's wife hands a small black pirate flag to each Raiders player as he steps off the bus. Leading the procession into the park's football stadium is the team mascot, a pirate. The Raiders march in lines of two, holding hands.

"Be calm," suggests an assistant coach. "Don't say a word. Let them feel the fear now. Let them hear those footsteps, boys."

Everything is first-class at the city championship. Instead of young volunteers, paid officials in black-and-white-striped uniforms work the chains and first-down markers. An electronic scoreboard is employed. Liberty City is officially the host program, even though no Warrior teams advanced this far. Sam Johnson mans a booth selling sodas, pickled red sausage, and chips. His assistant Daryl deep-fries potatoes and fish in a cauldron of oil. In the 95-pound championship game, Gwen Cherry easily defeats Overtown for the Bulls' second city championship in a row. Warriors coach Brian Johnson chose not to attend the game. Watching the Bulls win again would have been too painful, he said later.

Prior to the start of the 145-pound championship, the Raiders occupy an end zone for stretches and jumping jacks. While the team warms up, two men standing near the goalpost stare at Campos. One of the men is dressed in the Overtown colors of orange and green. The other wears Gwen Cherry colors, the visor of his baseball cap faces backward, and his sunglasses are tinted Bulls blue. They stare at Campos for more than a minute before he finally notices them. He knows what they want.

"You got ten grand?" Campos shouts over to them. The black lettering on the back of his T-shirt—"Mercy Rule in Effect"—bleeds through his oxford shirt. "Show me ten grand and we've got a bet. Let's see the money."

*   *   *

From "Winning it All" by Raul Campos, a section entitled "Responsibility":

"Let's talk about situations in which we experience personal or professional failure. The first step is accepting your role in the failure. You can't blame it all on fate. You can't fall victim to the notion that your failure was due totally to forces beyond your control, regardless of what they might have been. All this does is reinforce the theory that you have no control over your life and what happens to it—this is a theory that this entire book has tried to debunk. You create your own luck. You create what happens to you based on your decisions. You create your future both by your actions and your non-actions.

"We all fail sometimes. The question is: What do you do with that failure? Do you feel sorry for yourself? . . . While there's no question that you may not be able to control all circumstances, it is self-defeating and wrong to blame all failure on circumstances. A serious failure demands serious self-examination."

🏈 🏈 🏈

When it all ends, when Carl fails to score the tying touchdown in overtime, the Rattlers bench explodes onto a field instantly littered with orange jerseys and green polo shirts. Two Overtown linebackers dump a cooler of ice water on their coach's head.

"Please clear the field," bellows a voice over the PA system. "Please clear the field."

"They fucked us," spits Big Momma, the Raiders' assistant coach. Rain pours down on his head. "I hate to say it like that but they fucked us. I'm standing on the line. Carl broke the plane. They fucked us."

Carl scored a touchdown on the first play of regulation. Overtown managed to tie the score before halftime. In the second half, Palmetto's starting quarterback, who'd been running the offense for three straight years, went down with an injury. The offense never recovered, and never scored again. Regulation ended in a tie. For the second game in a row, the Raiders played a Kansas tie-breaker.

Overtown got the ball first, and the moment it scored a touchdown the heavens opened up. A cold rain drenched the playing field as the Raiders lined up for their four plays. First down. Second down. On third and three, Carl landed just short of the end zone. Campos raced down the sideline to argue that Carl had actually scored, but the referee, who was standing on the goal line during the play, upheld the original call. On fourth and three inches, needing nothing less than a touchdown, Carl was hit in the backfield for a loss. Overtown is city champion.

Campos grabs the oxygen tank, which rests on a cart with tiny rubber wheels, and rolls it back toward the bus. Cheerleaders heading to their less-luxurious school bus—the motor coach is for football players only—step through strewn athletic tape, crushed paper cups, and a pyramid of dirty pads. The team cruiser's blinking yellow hazard lights cut through the blackness. Campos consoles Carl, telling him there's no reason for him to cry because "nothing's gonna bring it back now." He kisses his wife, who wipes tears from her eyes.

"Heads up, men," he says to the boys changing near him. "We got nothing to be ashamed about. You guys did your jobs."

The used equipment is stuffed into the bus cargo hold. Coach Willy redistributes necklaces, bracelets, and earrings. Coach Lee paces back and forth, muttering about the officiating.

"That's all right," he says to the team. "When you guys get to the pros they be kissing your ass. Those refs be kissing your ass."

Campos stands with his arms crossed, leaning against the trunk of a Caprice parked near the bus. At Christmas he makes sure every Raider gets a small gift because he knows some of their families are too poor to buy presents. After every season he takes as many of the players as he can on field trips to see movies or to video game arcades or to the beach for picnics. He stays involved. When one player landed in jail, he bailed him out. On the day of the trial—the charges were eventually dropped—Campos sat in the back of the courtroom lending his support. Trick Daddy has called Campos more than once saying he doesn't know how to control his brother, Jarmaine, and would Campos have a talk with him? Campos knows a lot of his kids better than their parents do.

But he also promised them a trip to Disney World. And that trip isn't going to happen. A mother approaches him. Orlando was guaranteed, she reminds him; that's why she signed up with Palmetto in the first place. If she would have known that Palmetto couldn't get past sorry-assed Overtown she would have signed up her boy with Overtown instead.

"What's there to be depressed about it?" Campos replies. "What is there to be ashamed about? They just played in a championship game."

But playing in a local championship game and playing in Orlando for a national title are not the same thing. Campos would be the first to admit as much, if it were any other time.

"You one sorry-ass coach," the mother says. She turns to leave, turns back to say something, then reconsiders. "I'm still too upset so I'm not gonna even say what I really think of you. I'll just walk away."

The door to the bus opens with a whir of hydraulics. Campos climbs aboard and takes his customary seat in the first row. He doesn't talk to the Raiders as they file past. Eventually the door swings closed.

"That beer-bellied bastard!" the mother shouts, suddenly fortified for another barrage. "Like he's going anywhere with that bullshit." She rushes the bus and pounds on the door as the driver starts to pull away. Campos remains in his seat, alone.

"When we get through this season we will be the best youth football team to ever play the game," he'd said on the promotional videotape he made over the summer. "And I mean *ever*." Maybe it was the referees' fault. Maybe not. As Campos said on the tape, history cannot be changed.

Chapter 20

Orlando

Thanksgiving is the American holiday, in Miami as much as anywhere else. Miamians raise a toast of appreciation for their adopted homeland while serving up a side dish for their countries of origin. Cuban-Americans with black beans and rice, Colombian-Americans with roast pork. Brian Johnson's extended family this Thanksgiving will include several Bahamians. As is usually the case, the Warrior 95s' head coach has been asked to fry up a turkey. He'll stand in his mother-in-law's driveway for five hours heating the oil, injecting the bird with seasonings, and deep-frying everything until the bird's skin crisps to the touch and its meat achieves melt-in-your-mouth tenderness. With the turkey as the centerpiece, the Johnsons will chow down on sides of stuffing, homemade corn bread, pigeon peas and rice, potato salad, macaroni and cheese, collard greens—and ham, for anyone who, for some bizarre reason, balks at eating oil-infused poultry. On the Saturday before Thanksgiving, Miami is anticipating the holiday with a general feeling of goodwill.

"We got robbed, no doubt about it," grumbles Raul Campos, sitting atop a warped wooden plank in the bleachers of Curtis Park. He drove up this afternoon with two of his assistants. On the field are the same Overtown Rattlers who beat the Raiders last week. Today Overtown wins again, advancing to the regional playoffs. "We just wanted to see the injustice for ourselves," says Campos, standing up as the game ends, continuing a grumble he will carry long into Saturday night's regular poker game.

Brian Johnson of the Warriors sits in the stands with Beasley and Daryl, the head of football operations. Dion, the Warrior who overdosed on hot dogs earlier in the season, sits two rows down. Brian knows Dion doesn't have a father, so he brought him along to watch the first round of the state playoffs. Brian also brought along a small portable television so he can monitor his beloved University of Miami.

"What's the score now, B?" asks Daryl.

"Miami 33, Syracuse 0," Brian replies, same as he said three minutes ago. He looks down on the field. Two 110-pound teams are preparing to play the next game. He snickers. The visiting team, the Naples Hurricanes, has no chance.

Naples, Florida, is best known for its Swamp Buggy Races. The pioneers who founded Naples would storm the Everglades on jacked-up dune buggies. Usually they'd hunt deer, boar, and alligator. A couple of times a year they'd race each other on the Mile o'Mud, a submerged dirt track carved from a stand of pine trees. In the last twenty-five years most of the swamp buggies have been replaced by golf carts. Modern Naples crackles with all the energy of a retirement community, or, on a particularly electric day, a suburban shopping mall. As the Naples city champions, the Hurricanes won the privilege of crossing Alligator Alley to play Gwen Cherry. The winner advances to Jacksonville and then, with another victory, to Orlando and Disney World.

The Hurricanes appear ready to play. Prior to kickoff they gather in their end zone for warm-ups. Linebackers and running backs stand five feet apart from one another in rows militarily straight. On a coach's whistle they jump jacks in perfect synchronicity. Players hold their arms out like airplane wings, then bend over and touch their right fingers to their left cleats. Shiny white pants gleam on their legs. Waxed white helmets reflect the stadium lights, new stickers on every helmet. Their bright orange jerseys lack rips or grass stains. A platoon of Hurricane cheerleaders unfurls a paper banner for the players to tear through. With the first split of the banner coaches discharge fire extinguishers, bathing the players in a non-toxic cloud of white mist.

The 110-pound Gwen Cherry Bulls stand on their sideline, hands resting on hips, eyes transfixed by the spectacle. The Bulls do not perform calisthenics. The Bulls uniforms are basic blue-and-yellow hand-me-downs. Some of the players wear dented helmets with decals of a snorting bull. Some helmets lack decals altogether.

Final score: 22–0. All Bulls in a rout.

◆ ◆ ◆

In the years before the NFL built the rec center, youth football floundered at Gwen Cherry Park. Coaches recall scrambling for cash to pay bus drivers to haul teams to away games. Although money had been set aside to purchase both practice and game uniforms, the game jerseys never appeared. Several coaches say the teams' former administrator wore out his welcome in the community he served.

"He was going to get himself hurt," asserts coach A. D. Williams, who has worked at the park for a decade. "I mean, physically hurt. People were threatening him, driving by his house, accusing him of mismanaging the program and stealing funds."

The Boys & Girls Clubs took over the football program in August 1996. One young player showed up for the first practice with a loaded pistol. At the second practice, when a coach scolded one of his players, a pack of men watching from the sidelines stormed the field and physically attacked him. The park adopted the colors and nickname of the champion Northwestern Bulls. Not one Gwen Cherry Park team made the playoffs that first season.

The turnaround took only one season. In the second year, two Gwen Cherry teams advanced to the city championships. In the third year, 1999, the 95s won a national title. The administrators of other parks grumble that, thanks to the Boys & Girls Club, Gwen Cherry can charge less for football registration, meaning more talent gravitates there than to programs in Liberty City, Inner City, and Overtown.

On the day after Thanksgiving, the 110-pound Bulls, along with several sets of Gwen Cherry cheerleaders, board two motor coaches for the drive to Jacksonville. A few of these Bulls played on a Gwen Cherry team that won a national title two seasons ago. Most of the current Bulls have never before traveled beyond the Miami city limits.

"The first time I was outside of Miami was when I was ten and playing baseball for the Boys & Girls Club," says Charlie Brown, who oversees the football programs at Gwen Cherry and five other Miami parks. "We went to Tampa and you couldn't convince me it wasn't Germany or France or something. That's how different it felt. And it was just Tampa. But it was the first time I was out of Miami, and the world was opening up to me."

On I-95 heading north, vast sawgrass savannas are broken by golf course subdivisions and groves of bushy green trees heavy with grapefruit. "Leroy the Redneck Reindeer" plays on a radio, country music increasingly the only broadcast option. Minivans traveling to the Pop Warner cheerleading state finals, also held in Jacksonville this weekend, pass the bus. Soapy windows exhort "Honk If You're a Ram Fan," and "Go Erica and Brittany," and "Palm City Dolphins Cheerleaders #1." Around Daytona, as the country music yields to broadcasts of a NASCAR time trial, tall pines rise by the side of the highway. Elm trees past their autumn brilliance color the journey maroon and chocolate the rest of the way to the Diamond City.

Jacksonville, touching the Georgia border, feels more like a sister of Atlanta than it in any way resembles Miami. So quiet and clean is the city of one million people that Bull players refer to it as "country." Downtown is happily integrated on Friday night. Blacks and whites watch the holiday boat parade down the St. Johns River. Along the riverbank, visiting cheerleaders in sweat jackets and pleated skirts survey the procession of yachts through eyes dusted with glitter. The Bulls skip the parade, staying well outside down-town at a Hampton Inn, saving money by sleeping six to a suite.

Saturday dawns sunny and in the fifties, cold enough by Miami standards to require windbreakers and stocking caps. The Bulls play at a high school stadium against an undefeated team from sub-urban Jacksonville. As the Bulls introduce the team to defeat, mothers in blue-and-yellow sweatshirts taunt the Jacksonville boys suffering on the field. The cries of "Losers!" and "Country!" and the endless clanging of homemade noisemakers enrage a man wear-ing a Ralph Lauren polo shirt, khaki shorts, and Top-Siders.

"You should be ashamed of yourselves!" he shouts, facing the bleachers. "You should be ashamed!"

The mothers shake their noisemakers with increased vigor. Their boys are going to Orlando and his kid ain't.

"Go, Bulls!"

"Go, Bulls!"

Wayne Blanton, the executive director of the Greater Miami Boys & Girls Clubs, doesn't much care for the Pop Warner Super Bowl. On a Tuesday morning following the Jacksonville game, Blanton is dressed for manual labor. He's wearing a red T-shirt, jeans, work boots, and yellow leather gloves. Pine needles pierce his gray hair. Blanton has been running the Boys & Girls Club for twenty years, overseeing a $25 million budget. He also oversees fund-raising. Every year he hosts a celebrity auction at which fans bid on Alonzo Mourning's Miami Heat jersey or a signed White Sox jersey from local hero Jose Canseco. He also canvasses corporations for chari-table donations.

Of all the fund-raising efforts, nothing brings in more money annually than the Christmas tree sale, held in the club parking lot. Blanton's employment contract states that every year, from the week before Thanksgiving until Christmas, he is responsible for overseeing the delivery and subsequent sale of five thousand Fraser fir trees and fifteen hundred Scotch pine wreaths. He's just finished unloading a truckload of trees delivered from North Carolina. Blanton pulls off his gloves and throws them on the floor of his office, next to a bottle of shampoo, a pillow, and a sleeping bag. During Christmas tree season Blanton frequently spends the night on his office floor.

"We've got some big trees this year, but not as big as they were last year," he says, standing in front of his large wooden desk. His computer, which sits on a credenza behind him, is still covered in a terry-cloth towel to protect against the hurricane that never hit. "They're okay, I guess. As far as sales, we had a great Sunday but an average Saturday. It all depends on the weather."

He takes a phone call.

"Yeah, yeah," he says, shouting to be heard over the buzz from chain saws his workers are using to shape the trees. "I'm having trouble with them—they shorted me three thousand trees. These growers are getting so independent." An assistant pokes her head through the doorway to tell him that the office of former Dolphin quarterback Dan Marino is on line three. A man named Paul on line two wants three number-ten tree stands. Hanging on a wall near a poster celebrating the Boys & Girls Clubs' fiftieth anniversary is a framed photo of Blanton's son, an NBA alumnus, posing alongside basketball great Larry Bird.

The Boys & Girls Clubs started working with Gwen Cherry Park as a collaborative effort, Blanton says. The county runs the NFL recreation center, with its computers and after-school classes. Blanton's outfit runs the athletics and the summer sports programs. Gwen Cherry is just one of six parks managed by the Boys & Girls Clubs. In addition to football, most of those six parks also feature basketball, baseball, cheerleading, softball, and other activities.

"It's going to sound negative when I say this, but football is the most expensive program we run," Blanton says. "I'm afraid it might bankrupt our operation, as big as we are. We just sent three busloads of kids to Jacksonville. That cost us fifteen thousand dollars. We only have one team, Gwen Cherry, going to Orlando. Suppose we had six teams. What would we do then? I worry when the playoffs start. I try not to root against my own programs, but what am I going to do if six different teams make it to Orlando?"

A memo sent from Pop Warner's national office to Blanton, Liberty City's Sam Johnson, and the administrators of other parks reveals how a trip to the national championships can be priced beyond reach. In order to compete in the Super Bowl each player must stay at a Disney-owned hotel, at a minimum cost of $300 per player (and more for coaches and other adult chaperons). Every player must also purchase at least a handful of meal vouchers, at $11 apiece. The accommodations must be booked with Disney's sports travel agency, states the memo. The word "must" is underlined and in boldfaced type. In the past three years, Blanton has sent two teams to Orlando, at a cost of $23,000 per team.

"I'm down on the whole Super Bowl concept," Blanton says. "I think it's too much to give at an early age. I think kids should not be playing for a national championship, at least not before they are in high school. I'm not interested in rewarding the better kids at that young age—I'm interested in working with *all* the kids. I'd like to keep it local, like we do in baseball."

The Boys & Girls Clubs' baseball program is one of the finest in the country. It is not affiliated with Little League, so the teams never travel to Williamsport, Pennsylvania, to play in the Little League World Series. But, even without travel or national titles, top talent still emerges from Miami. As thanks for giving him his start in the game, Texas Ranger shortstop Alex Rodriguez donates a good-sized portion of his professional wages to Blanton and his operation.

"White teams in middle-class America use the Super Bowl as a social outing," Blanton says. "They can bear the costs. When it comes to the inner-city teams in our league, like Gwen Cherry or Liberty City or Overtown, it's a financial burden."

Outside the window, the chain saws whir and slice. Blanton reaches into a file cabinet and pulls out a few sheets of paper. It's a presentation he's working on, he says. He's preparing to ask his board of directors to drop football altogether.

● ● ●

The Bulls arrive in Orlando on Wednesday, the day of their national semifinal game against the Naperville Redskins from suburban Chicago. Charlie Brown, who works under Blanton at the Boys & Girls Clubs, successfully protested Pop Warner's policy requiring teams to stay on the Disney grounds. For a small additional fee paid to the national office, Gwen Cherry has been granted permission to stay in a hotel in Kissimmee. Brown selected the hotel not only for its low price but also because it has kitchens in which mothers traveling with the team can prepare meals.

"It's all good," says twelve-year-old linebacker Nicholas De La Cruz, emerging from the hotel pool on Thursday after the Bulls played their way into the title game with a two-touchdown victory over the previously undefeated and unscored-upon Redskins. "It's a long drive [from Miami to Orlando] and teachers gave us homework and stuff. But it was worth it, though. As soon as we got here we did it. The quicker you do your homework the more fun you have."

Besides swimming in the pool at the hotel, the players visit the Magic Kingdom theme park, their only visit to Disney proper. Charlie Brown does not take the team to Friday night's Pop Warner party at the MGM theme park. The entire park is closed off to the public, except for ticket-paying Pop Warner players, coaches, and family. There's no lines at the Voyage of the Little Mermaid or the Twilight Zone Tower of Terror. Vendors serve up free tacos and hot dogs. Pizza, soda, ice cream, popcorn—all of it, as much as anyone wants—is free.

"I saw the seventy-five-dollar ticket price on the itinerary and said 'Nope'," Brown explains. In lieu of the party, the Bulls watch a movie, followed by dinner at the Golden Corral, an all-you-can eat buffet restaurant. To most of the players, it's just as good.

Pop Warner teams that qualify for the national championship must pay their own way to Orlando, virtually disqualifying an inner-city team from, say, California. The teams that do come, at least the teams not from the East Coast, are almost uniformly suburban. The Bulls' opponent in the championship game, the Murrieta Valley Thunderhawks from Southern California, have lost only one game all year. And that, the team's boosters will tell anyone who asks, was by only three points. They came to Disney World by way of Arizona, where they won the Pop Warner western regional. The Murrieta players and their parents arrived in Orlando on Sunday, four days before their first game. They stayed in an official Disney hotel, the All-Star Sports Complex. With a full week in Orlando with only two games to play, the Thunderhawks visited all four Disney theme parks before Sunday's championship. The only thing the Murrieta players missed out on was the Pop Warner party at MGM, which they skipped as well.

"We saw that on the agenda but we decided not to go," said one Murrieta parent. "We put 'em all to bed by nine o'clock. We wanted them fresh and rested for the championship game."

A stiff wind inflates nylon tarps draped over the fence that rings the Disney field. Sunshine splatters through clouds that race past as if they were late for an appointment in Daytona Beach. A press box hovers twenty feet above midfield. Weaved into the scaffolding are banners advertising various Pop Warner sponsors, including Reebok and U.S. Airways. One banner promotes the Pop Warner MasterCard—a 4.9 percent interest rate and no annual fee. A disembodied voice booms out the names of the starting lineup.

◆ ◆ ◆

Up in the press box, Jon Butler addresses a walkie-talkie. He is the executive director of Pop Warner Little Scholars, Inc., the national office. He's wearing a blue blazer over a white polo and khaki pants; his curly brown hair juts away from his ears. He took over as the main man at Pop Warner four years ago, following a career as an athletic apparel retailer. From the press box he sees a flawless playing field ringed by bleachers packed with fans. ESPN cameramen prowl the grounds. In a Disney field house behind Butler, sixty-four teams of cheerleaders jump and twirl to Britney Spears songs, trying to bring home Pop Warner national championships of their own.

The championships have been held at Disney for six years. Every year the event becomes a little more flashy, and the coverage on television and in the press a little thicker. Pop Warner people like Butler are trying to hike a path blazed by Little League baseball. The World Series of that youth sport is covered in *Sports Illustrated* and *ESPN* magazine. The championship game is broadcast on ABC-TV. Pop Warner is doing its best to emulate: ESPN coverage of the 145-pound championship; Disney and national sponsorships. It's a healthy start, at least from Butler's perspective.

"This gives us great exposure for our product," Butler says. Since the Super Bowl moved to Orlando and, more important, since it debuted on ESPN, Pop Warner has secured those corporate partnerships with the likes of Reebok and U.S. Airways. To Pop Warner—a for-profit company—that's a big deal.

"I think there's a downside to our system," Butler admits. "On one hand, the Super Bowl trip provides a positive reward for good play, while on the other hand, yes, it does prompt some people to lose focus on what Pop Warner is supposed to be all about. I think that's reality. It's the way it is."

When discussing the purpose of Pop Warner, Butler speaks as if quoting from a press release. He notes that the league emphasizes teamwork by refusing to track the personal statistics of its players. The main goal of Pop Warner, he says, is to use football (and cheerleading) to "develop strong, smart, responsible, healthy young men and women." Discipline is instilled. Egos are checked. Sportsmanship is preached to the increasing number of parents who "take a child's game too seriously."

"From all the psychological studies that I've read, and from the psychologists that I've talked to, I would argue that at our age range winning is much more important to the adults than to the kids," Butler says. "The kids can lose some real close games, yet fifteen or twenty minutes later they are all over at the concession stand sharing Cokes and hot dogs."

Butler insists that with kids between the ages of six and fourteen, the best team record is about 6–4. The players win enough to taste the thrill and satisfaction of winning, but lose enough to understand that life goes on.

"I don't want to sound insincere or smart-alecky, but the kids are almost always right," Butler says. "The adults are the ones that abuse the system or create values that we wish weren't there."

● ● ●

So many Murrieta parents have traveled cross-country for the Super Bowl that they overflow their small set of bleachers. Men in black-and-red T-shirts hang their arms over the fence. Mothers broadcast pregame predictions into cell phones. Their boys stretch on the bright green field, so flat and pristine it could be a putting green. The Murrieta players' names are sewn onto the back of their uniforms, which are as black as their helmets. Stuck on the sides of each helmet is a red logo of an irate bird.

"Tweeet!" With a blast of his whistle, Murrieta's head coach calls for a team huddle. His players gather in a white tent erected in a corner of the north end zone. A homemade felt banner hangs over the opening of the tent: "Thunderhawks: Who's next?"

"If we want to give them a good game then we got to play hard," instructs the coach. Although pregame is the customary time for a pep infusion, there is a sense of hopelessness in the coach's voice. He is not barking in Vince Lombardi mode. The veins on his neck remain recessed. Despite the cockiness of the felt banner hanging over the tent, the coach seems to know what's in store for his players this afternoon. "Be on top of your game," he says, looking from face mask to face mask to face mask. "Try your best."

The Gwen Cherry crowd, comparatively, isn't very large, most likely because the high school team upon which the Bulls are styled, Miami Northwestern, will be playing in the state title game tonight in Tallahassee, three hours north. Those who've traveled to Orlando for the lesser championship game counter the Murrieta cheering section as best they can. Air horns punctuate the names of each Gwen Cherry player announced over the loudspeakers. One woman rattles a noisemaker constructed from an empty plastic water bottle and a few small rocks. Commissioner Mark Peterson stands near the Bull bleachers, his hands clasped behind his back. He's here on the off chance there may be some problem he needs to solve. He can't imagine what that would be, and he's not planning to do much of anything.

"Am I sick of football?" he asks rhetorically, sixteen weeks into the season. "Oh, yeah."

The Bulls sport white jerseys with blue pants. Their yellow helmets remain festooned with mismatched Bull logos. Some helmets lack logos altogether. In his pregame speech, Bulls head coach Daron Chiverton seems as dispassionate as his opponent.

"All he said was to stay focused," reports Tevin Gibson, a thirteen-year-old fullback applying dabs of eye-black to each cheek. "He said every game is a big game, and that we should go over everything we preached. It's always going to get real ugly, he said, but that's just our word. That's what we say every time."

Did Coach express any fear about the Thunderhawks?

"Nope."

Did the coach say anything at all about them?

"Not really."

The score after two quarters: 13–0, Bulls.

"You guys still want to play some football?" barks the Murrieta coach, back in his tent at halftime.

"Yes, sir!"

"It's never over till it's over, you guys understand that? It's never over till it's over!"

On the first play of the second half, the Bulls return the kick-off eighty yards for a touchdown. The boy who scores the touchdown does not spike the ball, nor does he celebrate in any way. No Bull congratulates him except for a casual "Way to go" tossed by an assistant coach. The face masks on Murrieta's shiny black helmets aim down at the ground. Parents' attitudes shift into resignation.

"Second place in the whole country, that's pretty good," says one mother into her cell phone. "I think that's pretty good."

Final score: 27–0.

"Congratulations to the Gwen Cherry Bulls out of Miami," bellows the press box announcer.

The Gwen Cherry fans rattle noisemakers and synchronize a blast of two air horns. Hugs are passed from one player to another. Coach Daron Chiverton holds aloft a large wooden plaque engraved with the words "National Champions." Each player receives a medallion on a red-white-and-blue ribbon. For fullback Tevin Gibson it's his second national championship medal.

"We just wanted to get out here," he says of his team's businesslike dismissal of Murrieta Valley. The sun and sweat of the game cause his once-fresh eye-black to run down his cheeks. "We just felt like we're hungry. We just wanted to get out here and do our business and go."

On the other sideline, parents do their best to buck up the spirits of the vanquished Thunderhawks.

"Move out there, boys. We got here, baby, it's all right."

After imparting a few words of consolation, and after thanking everyone for a good season, the coach announces the itinerary for the night: The players are heading back to the Magic Kingdom for yet one more crack at Space Mountain. The parents will party at the House of Blues. Twelve-year-old Thunderhawk Kirk Petty walks with his mother toward the parking lot. Her arm rests around his padded neck.

"They're really fast," he says of the Bulls.

Chapter 21

Awards Banquet

Winter in Miami is a fleeting season. On New Year's Eve the mercury might drop into the forties. Morning joggers can see their breath into February. For a populace conditioned to heat, even a somewhat arctic blast is tough to take. The water in swimming pools ripples in the breeze. Bare toes refuse to take the ocean's temperature. It's cold, relatively.

And then it's over. By March the weather again grows so hot that savvy Miamians tote umbrellas to block the sun's glare. Spring-breakers are pitied as they roast in convertibles. By April the full fury of summer is unleashed. The sky this mid-April morning is blue and clear enough to raise the temperature into the nineties. As the heat rises off the parking lot of Northwestern High School, young men in ties and dress pants, vests and their shiniest black shoes sprint into the school's auditorium. Inside, atop curved white walls, metal air-conditioning ducts pump out cool relief.

"Hey man, how you doin', baby? Good to see you. Good to see you." Coach Brian Johnson slaps palms as his Warriors plop into padded blue seats. His sunglasses hang from the collar of a shirt with a polo player stitched on the pocket. The rest of the 95-pound Warrior coaches huddle around Brian. Beasley tells Pete about the coaching clinic he and Brian attended yesterday, the one hosted by the new head coach at the University of Florida. They learned new ways to tackle, the UM running back coach was there—it was amazing. McAdoo the street agent sits near the stage, his black Kangol cap worn backward. Even before the ceremony begins he's snapping pictures of coaches and players.

Every spring the Warriors set aside a day to honor the participants in all the organization's programs: baseball, basketball, girls' softball, football, and cheerleading. Brian and Beasley worked the phones to make sure their football players showed up. Most of them did: Antwan, the twins, Stevie. Phillip is not here. Neither is Diamond.

"We called him a dozen times, but his mom wouldn't answer," Beasley reports.

Prepubescent squeals bounce around the room. The talk is of video games and new outfits. Stevie hops on his seat, telling everyone he's going to win the defensive MVP award. Antwane lounges with his legs flared, his feet laced into spotless Reebok sneakers, his torso cloaked in Tommy Hilfiger. DaQuan is ordered to remove his red velour visor when indoors.

"Is there someone here from the Northwestern maintenance department?" booms a voice over the PA. Holding the banquet at Northwestern is a coup for the school. By establishing a relationship with the young football players now there's a better chance that, when they select the high school where they'll play ball, Northwestern will be their first choice. "Can someone from the Northwestern maintenance department please turn on the lights on the stage? Hello?"

Kliegs go on to reveal a gleaming treasure. Eleven tables draped in gold bunting dominate the stage. On the tables stand more than a thousand trophies of plastic men with muscular, outstretched arms. It's as if a drug house had been raided and its contents displayed for the press. Behind the tables stand four golden palm trees planted atop Greek columns. A black ribbon hangs on each tree, signifying Warrior Pride.

Sam steps to the microphone to thank everyone for turning out. An assistant from the staff of County Commissioner Barbara Carey-Shuler takes over when he surrenders the podium.

"We need programs like this Optimist program here so children have a place to go after school as opposed to standing on the street doing things inappropriate for their age," she says in a government-issue monotone.

The Warriors operate with the help of private donations, federal grants, and any other funding Sam can find. County money, Sam says, is the foundation, the main capital for shoulder pads and basketballs and plastic cheerleader pom-poms. Until recently. In January, Miami-Dade county commissioners slashed the grant to the Liberty City Optimist Club in half. On top of that, the City of Miami proper, under its new mayor, reduced its donation to the Optimists by 20 percent. Almost every nonprofit program serving Liberty City, from welfare retraining to after-school tutoring, suffered cuts. Out of necessity, Sam laid off his two employees.

"This is one of the largest Optimist programs in the county," the bureaucrat continues, sweeping her arm from one end of the auditorium to the other. "We are hoping it will succeed for ever and ever, but, as you know, it is no longer receiving a hundred percent of the funding. So you are all going to have to help Sam raise money. You have to support Sam. You have to be involved in the policy process.

"On the Dade County commission there are four black commissioners and nine Hispanic commissioners," she says, pausing as if setting up a punch line. She is black, as is the community she represents. "Now, where do you suppose all the money goes?"

*   *   *

When the last trophy lands in the last pair of young hands, the audience moves into the school cafeteria for a banquet. Caterers dole out baked chicken, wax beans, yellow rice, potato pie, and, to drink, sugary red Kool-Aid.

"That's a crack baby," McAdoo tells Brian while tearing into a chicken leg. He's talking about a Warrior safety, who threw down his participation trophy when someone else was named defensive MVP. "I know the mother. He on Ritalin. How you say it . . . he too hyper, he a crack baby. I know. That's how crack babies behave."

A box of trophies sits on a chair next to McAdoo. He purchased them himself, to hand to every Warriors coach. Additionally, McAdoo's drawn up certificates of appreciation for the two assistants let go by Sam.

"I'm down with all the parks," McAdoo says. "But my son, he's going back to the Warriors. They get it. They don't let someone coach if they going to run around celebrating themselves. If their team score a touchdown the coach ain't running onto the field screaming. It's the closest park to my house, it's my neighborhood park, but ultimately I'm down with Sam."

He pulls an oversized black button out of his bag. It's another curious homemade creation, dubious in its value yet extraordinary in its sentiment of affection and respect. Printed on the button in yellow letters are the words: "Sam: Hall of Fame."

The 95-pound coaches sit together, already hatching plans for next season. Pete and Beasley have been meeting at Brian's house every week since the season ended. The Georgia Southern offense that fell into such disfavor has been scrapped for a whole new system. Next year the Warriors will use the same offense employed by Apopka High School, the team from Orlando that upset Northwestern to win the state title. Brian found the Apopka system on the Internet, his usual source of such information.

"This year we're going to start early," he says. "When I say 'start early' I mean as a coaching staff. I'm talking about everybody that's been involved with us as far as making sure we got the proper kids and stuff. We going to try and make something happen on our own. It's not like we're going recruiting or anything like that, but we're going to try and bring some kids here, man."

As they eat their food and imagine their futures, Brian and his assistants have no idea how the 2002 season will actually unfold. They are unaware that by the time practice starts next season a family from the Dominican Republic will move into one of the houses facing Hadley Park, or that the name of the school on the Hadley Park property will change from Allapattah Middle to Lenora Braynon Middle.

"They changed the name of the damn school," McAdoo will report. Although Braynon, who died in 1970, was the first black to be named Florida's Teacher of the Year, McAdoo and others will assume her name is Hispanic. "I look up there the other night and I'm tripping. They moving us out of here. But I'm going to die with the community. I'm going to die right here. I'm not going nowhere."

Janet Reno will lose the Democratic primary for governor. The election, which will be decided by less than 9,000 votes, will be marred by charges of black disenfranchisement. Dozens of precincts in Miami will open for voting hours later than scheduled. In Liberty City, a Reno stronghold, new electronic machines designed to eliminate the hanging-chad problems of the 2000 presidential election will break down for hours. Governor Jeb Bush will declare a state of emergency and extend voting hours, but many poll workers will refuse to stay longer.

The players on Raul Campos's 145-pound Palmetto Raiders will age out of Pop Warner. It's Campos's custom to bounce back down to the 110s, take on another group of players, and stay with them for three seasons until they, too, age out. In 2002, the Palmetto 110s will finish undefeated in regular-season play. They'll also avoid a loss in the playoffs, winning the city championship. Eventually they will march to Orlando to play in the Pop Warner Super Bowl. It will be a great season for Palmetto and a great season for the team's coach.

Campos won't be that coach. When the 2001 season ends and he asks to take over the Palmetto 110s, he assumes the coach assigned to the team will step aside for him. After all, he's a two-time national champion, the greatest coach of youth football there has ever been. The incumbent has other ideas. The incoming 110s are loaded with talent—they're the same 95-pounders who destroyed the Warriors in the game Brian Johnson left in an ambulance. The sitting coach feels he can take the team to Orlando on his own, thank you. And he will be proven right.

"It's all politics over there," Coach Brown will grumble. Brown, like most of Campos's assistants at Palmetto, will follow his boss to

Tamiami, Campos's third home park in four years. "It makes no sense to me. Why would you favor a coach who has never won anything over a coach like Campos who is a national champion? It's politics and favoritism."

The Tamiami Colts have long fielded weak teams. The program's location in the primarily Cuban—and baseball-mad—western suburbs isolates it from the black talent pool. But, in a practice prior to the first game of the 2002 season, an imported black quarterback will hand off to a speedy black running back, also imported. On green grass mowed in a checkerboard pattern, Campos will teach his recruits the same plays the 145s employed at Palmetto. It's the same system Campos has been using for years.

With his imported talent, Campos's Colts will start strong, beating Liberty City 29–0 in the first game of the season. But his shallow bench will catch up with him. Over the course of the season, the Colts will lose more games than they win. Campos will be suspended for a game after arguing with a referee. As the Palmetto 110s march to Orlando, Campos's team will fail to make the playoffs. He still won't be able to find a publisher for his autobiography.

Prior to the start of the season, Gator Rebhan will drop his lawsuit against Pop Warner. The suspension will expire anyway, negating his need to follow through in court. Rebhan will return as the head coach of the 145-pound Suniland Sundevils. His one-year absence may have hurt his recruiting efforts: Suniland will fail to advance to the city championships.

Sixty kids will show up for the Liberty City Warriors' first practice, giving Brian twice as much talent to choose from as the year before. By the first kickoff, the team will look, simply, great. The 95s will beat Tamiami, 29–6. Then Richmond, 6–0. Then Suniland, 6–0.

"This is the year to follow the Warriors," Coach Pete will exclaim at a practice. "We looking hellified."

At that practice, Diamond Pless will drag a ball carrier to the ground behind the line of scrimmage. A cloud of dust will rise from the field as the halfback accepts his loss of yardage. In the first four games of the new season, Diamond will emerge as the best defender on a skilled defensive team.

"Diamond, he a terrier!" declares Coach Pete. "We working on his leadership and stuff but he's the best one on the D. He play a little still; we working on that, we trying to get him to take this all serious. But he the best one. The Diamond that showed up this year, he for real, know what I'm saying?"

What starts out as a dream season will begin to crumble at the Gwen Cherry game, which the Warriors will lose by a touchdown. The Liberty City parents will excoriate Coach Beasley for his inability to manufacture a touchdown for the third game in a row. After the game Diamond won't seem too upset.

"I played all right," he'll say, settling into a lunch of a junior bacon cheeseburger, french fries, and a tall cup of fruit punch. "Our offense need to score more, that's all it is."

Diamond will continue talking to his imprisoned father, though the calls will taper off from once a week to once every two Saturdays or so. A grown friend of Diamond's mother will show Diamond a few card tricks. As he shuffles the cards, the man will look down at Diamond and say, "Boy, you look just like a friend of mine." The resemblance will be so strong that the man will call his friend on the phone and tell him to get down to his place, quick. When the friend arrives, Diamond will meet his birth father for the first time.

"I didn't even know I had another father," Diamond will say, chomping a fry as if his teeth were pulping a bolt of lumber. "My momma says they always be fussing and stuff. When I told her that my father says he's going to buy me a scooter on my birthday when I turn twelve, she laughed and said it ain't ever gonna happen. He told me he was going to move into a new place so we could be together, and my momma, she laughed at that, too."

Diamond won't ever again show up for another practice, or for another game. Officially, he'll have quit. More accurately, his mother will have made him quit. The coaches won't know why. During a home game against West Kendall, the black mesh bag of jerseys will sit on the sidelines near an orange cooler filled with water. Diamond's 33 will be the only jersey in the bag.

"I went to his mother and talked to her about keeping him on the team," Brian will say. "This lady know what's going on. It's not like she don't know. It's a waste of fucking time trying to help people that don't want the help."

Without Diamond, the Warriors defense will grow porous. Cream puff West Kendall will score a late touchdown to force a 6–6 tie. A week later, following a loss to the Northwest Falcons, the entire defensive coaching staff—Pete, Chico, Tubbs, and even Brian's own brother, who will join the team as an assistant—will quit the team to protest Beasley's offensive ineptitude.

"My own brother walked out on me," Brian will complain. "My own goddamn brother. It made me rethink that whole 'blood is thicker than water' business, that's for sure."

Still, there will be playoffs for the Warriors at the end of the year—first round and out. An improvement, though no Orlando. The University of Miami will play in another national championship game. The Dolphins will collapse late in their season, as usual. Yet another team from Miami, Norland High, will win the state championship. Football in Miami will go on, though without Brian.

"Man," he will say, "I am done coaching football in Miami. Done. I am DONE. Done, done, done, done, done. *Done.*

"Coaching the Warriors has become a problem for me. I have no feeling for it no more. I don't want to be fucking bothered, to be honest. At the end of nine years I learned, for one, that everybody's not your friend. You can depend upon only a handful of people—that's it. The rest of the people out there, they worthless, they have no meaning or nothing. They just out there.

"I don't have no feelings now. I know I gave it all I had. Youth football in Miami . . . it's a good thing to keep kids involved, but it's not about the kids anymore. It's about something else, and that something ain't the kids."

But that's the future. Now, at the banquet, Brian exudes only optimism. And hunger. After he finishes a second plate of chicken and downs a third cup of Kool-Aid, he heads back to the buffet for dessert. He tosses onto the table the awards program he'd been reading. It lands faceup. There's the list of speakers, a thank-you to the caterers, and a personal message from Sam recognizing everyone as "winners on and off the field." A small note at the bottom: "Football registration begins again in two weeks." The yellow sandwich board stands in the grass across from Hadley Park.

As if everyone doesn't already know. As if everyone isn't already waiting.

Acknowledgments

In addition to everyone associated with Pop Warner football in Miami, I wish to thank Brendan Cahill, Jane Caporelli and the staff of the Miami River Inn, Jim DeFede, Steve Dudley, Morgan Entrekin, Ashley Fantz, Paul George, Ted B. Kissell, Kent Lam, John Lombardi, Todd Lubin, Daniel Maurer, Kirk Nielsen, Kirk Semple, Janine Sieja, Rebecca Wakefield, and Amy Williams. Although I consulted many histories of Miami, I was most influenced by the works of Marvin Dunn and Raymond A. Mohl, whom I thank. The Florida Room at the Miami-Dade Public Library helped with fact checking. This book evolved from an article published in Miami *New Times* and included in the anthology *Best American Sports Writing*. Tom Finkel encouraged the original story, then edited it expertly. Special thanks to my family, particularly Melanie Rose Umbdenstock. Thanks above all to Steve Almond.